Shaping U.S.-China Relations

Shaping U.S.-China Relations

A Long-Term Strategy

A Council on Foreign Relations Study Group Report

Michel Oksenberg
Elizabeth Economy

The Council on Foreign Relations, Inc., is a nonprofit, nonpartisan membership organization dedicated to promoting improved understanding of international affairs through the free and civil exchange of ideas.

For further information about the Council or this Report, please contact the Public Affairs Office, Council on Foreign Relations, 58 East 68th Street, New York, NY 10021.

CONTENTS

ACKNOWLEDGMENTS

We would like to thank Nancy Yao from the Council on Foreign Relations for her research and logistical assistance and Sarah Holmes from Stanford University for her research and administrative support.

We also want to express our appreciation to the members of the Council's China and Constructive Engagement Study Group. The Study Group's participants, especially those who wrote papers, provided much of the data and many of the insights for this report.

Finally, we wish to thank the Amoco Corporation for sponsoring this China project, including a series of meetings and papers over the past year. As always, opinions expressed in Council on Foreign Relations reports are those of the writers alone and are not necessarily shared by the sponsor.

INTRODUCTION

The rise of China in world affairs is a major feature of our era. An increasingly contentious debate has erupted in the United States over how to respond to this development. Figuring out a successful policy toward China is no easy task, but any sound strategy must be rooted in a sense of history.

The death of Deng Xiaoping, the visits to China by Vice President Gore and President Clinton, a reciprocal state visit to Washington, the reversion of Hong Kong to Chinese rule on July 1, 1997, the convening of a Party Congress in late 1997, and a new National People's Congress in early 1998 guarantee that China and U.S. policy toward it will attract scrutiny in 1997–98. In anticipation of these events, voices are already calling for a reappraisal of a policy adopted only a year ago.

A sure recipe for a failed policy would be to base America's approach toward China on either the events of the last weeks or even the last few years or on unproved fears or hopes about the future. The most sensible perspective would consider the last 25 years, the period during which China has emerged or re-emerged into Asia and the world as a major power. During that period, the leaders of China and the industrial democracies have sought to establish a mutually satisfactory framework for peacefully integrating China into the evolving international security, economic, and political systems. And the core question is whether basically to persist on the path pursued since 1971.

China and America each find their relations with the other wanting. Both realize that the toughest problems between them lie ahead. But over the last 25 years, both countries have made enormous strides toward better understanding of the other and better management of conflicting interests.

Actually, the participants in the rolling American debate about policy toward China agree on many points. They see China as a major power in Asia and potentially in the world. They believe that China's emergence on the world's stage will inevitably change the international system, just as occurred in the late 19th and early 20th centuries when Germany, Japan, Russia, and the United States rose to challenge the leadership of Britain and France. And they agree that no relationship will be more important to American security and economic interests in the years ahead than that with China.

The nub of the often vitriolic disagreement is the question of whether Chinese and American interests are fundamentally at odds or whether the two sides can reduce their differences to manageable proportions. The alarmists argue that China will inevitably pose a military threat in the Asia-Pacific region, that it cannot be trusted to adhere to its international agreements, and that it will continue to hold positions on matters such as human rights and economics that are deeply at variance with American values and interests. The optimists contend that, despite the wide-ranging differences with China, the country's inclusion in the international system that began 25 years ago has been, on balance, good for the United States, China, China's neighbors, and the world, and that further immersion will further improve matters. On this basic argument, the evidence supports the optimists, and the optimists appear more realistic than the alarmists.

Realism, rooted in a sense of history, provides a sound basis for a coherent U.S. policy toward China. The policy recommended by the alarmists—to concentrate on and prepare for the inevitable Sino-American confrontation—is neither justified nor workable. It is not justified because on balance China has contributed more to American interests than it has harmed them. It is not workable because the American public and U.S. friends and allies around the world are unprepared to bear the costs such an enterprise would entail.

A historical perspective clears away a good deal of political flak and underbrush. It reveals the areas of Chinese recalcitrance, such as civil rights or weapons sales and purchases. But it also permits us to see the progress that has been made and the potential for further improvement. It helps reveal both the continuity of Beijing's foreign policy goals, strategy, and tactics and the degree to which China has adapted its domestic institutions and policies to the demands of the international community. It also allows us to determine how China can be integrated into the international system peacefully and with mutual respect. Such integration should be the overriding American strategic goal. Perhaps most important, the historical perspective encourages us to be less frantic; not to bide our time but to take our time.

In 25 years China has gone from a pariah state to a generally responsible member of the international community, mostly because of its own decisions but with significant help from the rest of the world. There is still a very long way to go before China is fully integrated into the world community. In many respects, China does not appear capable of shouldering the responsibilities that extensive involvement in international affairs entails. Most important, the absence of the rule of law has been a serious impediment to China's fulfillment of its commitments to the rest of the world. But looking back 25 years, what is striking is how much progress China has made.

The United States must work to ensure that this progress continues. We make four recommendations:

First, the United States must establish a set of priorities with the People's Republic of China that contributes to PRC integration into the world community and serve as a benchmark for the relationship. These priorities should be in the areas of security, economic relations, and development of the rule of law. They will also help identify more specific objectives for U.S. participation with China in international regimes, such as encouraging Chinese adherence to the standards of the International Atomic Energy Agency and the Missile Technology Control Regime, securing Chinese membership in the World Trade Organization on terms that protect a liberal trade regime, and promoting the development of rule of law through institution building.

Second, the United States needs to build up areas of common interest with China, even as individual problems continue to crop up in the relationship. Just as trade and arms control served as cornerstones of the U.S.-Soviet relationship and buffered the rancorous debates over human rights or Afghanistan, Washington and Beijing should pursue the most promising areas of cooperation, including preservation of stability on the Korean peninsula , environmental protection, energy conservation, improvement of China's monetary and financial system, and institutional development.

Third, China must have a seat at the table when the rules that affect its interests are decided. Twice in this century, after World War I and World War II, China did not participate in establishing regional security arrangements. Others made decisions that adversely affected China's interests, stimulating Chinese nationalism and defiance of the arrangements. This mistake should not be repeated.

Fourth, the United States must consult extensively with its European and Asian partners about China. The United States needs the support of Europe and Asia in establishing a set of norms and institutions that will govern China's and America's interaction in world affairs. While our study reveals that on many issues cooperation will be difficult to achieve, rule making and norm building is a multilateral process. The United States can lead but it cannot dictate.

We deliberately say little about Taiwan, clearly one of the most important issues in Sino-American relations. The Council has already sponsored a major policy statement on Taiwan by an independent group that both authors signed. That statement underscored the U.S. interest in the continued stability, prosperity, and freedom of the people of Taiwan and emphasized the American obligation—written into law through the Taiwan Relations Act—to assist Taiwan in maintaining its ability to deter an unprovoked attack. We return briefly to U.S. policy toward Taiwan in our conclusion. But our approach is rooted in the view that Taiwan's future is best secured in the context of constructive relations among all the major powers of the region, especially China, Japan, and the United States. Our focus, therefore, is on relations among the major powers of Asia, recognizing that the preservation of their currently good relations is the best guarantee for continued stability in Asia.

Finally, none of these recommendations can be attained without strong presidential leadership. The president must vigorously articulate his strategy toward China and East Asia more broadly and build the kind of bipartisan support for a long-term approach that can withstand the ups and downs that are bound to occur in Sino-

American relations. The point is for the president to fashion a political base sufficient to keep his long-term strategy on track. President Clinton's lengthy remarks about China in his 1997 State of the Union Address are an example of the leadership that is required. Only through presidential intervention can the entire administration speak in a coherent and constructive voice. In addition, among the president's chief advisers—the national security adviser and the secretary or assistant secretaries of state—someone must assume the lead for articulating and coordinating Asia and China policy. Without these measures, administration policy will simply be a cacophony of sounds.

THE COURSE OF CHINA'S PARTICIPATION

Chinese involvement in international affairs over the past two decades consists of three dimensions: 1) its formal accession to international agreements and accords and its membership in international organizations; 2) its creation of domestic political and economic institutions to implement its commitments; 3) and its policies and behavior. We now assess China's record in each of these.

Formal Accession

In every area, Chinese involvement in international regimes has grown rapidly. Indeed, it is difficult to recall the extent of China's isolation 25 years ago. The People's Republic had just gained the China seat in the United Nations and hence had not yet become a member of its principal organizations. Foreign trade accounted for less than five percent of GNP, and the United States trade embargo had just been lifted. Telecommunications and transportation links between China and the rest of the world were few and indirect. The principal method of entry was by train from Hong Kong to the border, then a walk across Lowu bridge, a slow train ride to Canton, and finally a flight to Beijing on a Russian turboprop plane. There were no direct flights between the mainland and Tokyo, Seoul, Hong Kong, or any Association of Southeast Asian Nations (ASEAN) capital. Few Chinese students studied abroad. As late as 1977, foreign businessmen were largely confined to the semiannual Canton Trade Fair. So few foreigners traveled to China that foreign governments recorded and disseminated a monthly list of all foreign delegations and individuals who visited China. China's leaders vilified international arms control agreements and the international economic system. China assumed a defiant posture toward both the United States and the Soviet Union.

All this has changed. China has rejoined the world. No aspect of world affairs is exempt from its influence. To those familiar with the China of the 1930s and late 1940s, the country's performance is not totally surprising. It has resumed the development trajectory it was on before the Japanese invasion and the civil war, although development now is more rapid and more extensive. To Westerners whose personal involvement with the country began during its days of isolation from the late 1950s to the early 1970s, the change over the past 25 years is extraordinary, testament to the wisdom of extending a welcoming hand to China. But to those whose experience is limited to the last ten years, the progress is less striking, and the persistence of obstacles is the more evident aspect of China's performance. One sees the glass of water as half full or half empty depending on when one first saw the glass.

Objectively, however, the number of international accords and organizations to which China is now a party is staggering. For example, within the United Nations system, China's membership in international governmental organizations has grown from 21 in 1977 to 49 in 1995, while its participation in international nongovernmental organizations skyrocketed from 71 in 1977 to 1,013 in 1995.

In the realm of the international economy, the growth of China's involvement has been similarly impressive. By any formal measure, participation has soared. Total foreign trade rose from $21 billion in 1978 to $73.8 billion in 1986 to $280 billion in 1995, increasing from 14 percent of GNP in 1978 to 31 percent in 1986 to 56 percent in 1995.[1] Moreover, the total number of pledged joint venture projects leaped from 922 in 1982 to more than 250,000 in 1995, with over 150,000 commitments in 1993–95 alone. China is also investing abroad: by 1994, its cumulative foreign direct investment totaled $16 billion.[2]

Similarly, in the trade and investment arena, including such issue-specific regimes as telecommunications, civil aviation, and energy, China has become a player of global importance. China secured observer status at the General Agreement on Tariffs and Trade in 1982, became a permanent observer in 1984, and applied for full membership in GATT in 1986. After protracted negotiations, full membership in the World Trade Organization (WTO), GATT's successor, appears to be within reach. China is also a member of the Asia Pacific Economic Cooperation (APEC) process and its several working groups. It has also entered the world intellectual property rights regime, joining the World Intellectual Property Organization in 1980, the Paris Convention on intellectual property rights protection in 1984, and the Berne Convention on protection of literature and the arts in 1992.

In banking and finance, China joined the World Bank and International Monetary Fund (IMF) in 1980, accepted the 1992 Basle Capital Accord as the standard for capital adequacy for its own banks, and joined the Bank for International Settlements in 1996. China is the World Bank's largest borrower and one of the largest recipients of bilateral development assistance from advanced industrial economies. Moreover, it has become a significant commercial borrower and is one of only three transition economies with an investment-grade credit rating on its sovereign external debt. As a further indication of its stature and performance, it had accumulated over $100 billion in foreign currency reserves by late 1996, had issued $8.75 billion in debt instruments from 1991 to mid-1995, $5.6 billion in equity issues in international capital markets, and by the end of 1995 had an external debt of $120 billion, 40 percent derived from international financial institutions and bilateral government loans and 60 percent from commercial banks and private creditors. China's four major state-owned banks—the Bank of China, the Industrial and Commercial Bank, the Agricultural Bank of China, and the Construction Bank of China—all seek to expand their operations overseas. Furthermore, China has taken the first halting steps in opening its banking, insurance, and financial service industries to foreign competition by allowing select foreign firms to sell insurance in Shanghai.

Developments in telecommunications have been no less rapid. The People's Republic assumed the China seat in the International Telecommunication Union in 1971. Since then, it has been sensitive to the evolution of GATT principles, enjoying observer status in the Negotiating Group on Basic Telecommunications and participating in the APEC Telecommunications Working Group. Perhaps even more impressive has been China's interaction with private sector telecommunications equipment manufacturers and service providers outside the ITU context. Corporations such as

Hughes, AT&T, Motorola, NEC, Siemens, Hong Kong Telecom, and Hitachi have become major actors in the Chinese market, with joint venture manufacturing of switching equipment, fiber optic cable, satellite equipment, and computers that together constitute the telecommunications transformation. Fiber optic cables now link Shanghai to Japan and beyond and connect Hong Kong to East and Southeast Asia and beyond. Circuits to the United States carried by the Ministry of Post and Telecommunications and AT&T alone have increased from 220 in 1989 to 1,908 in 1995.

Civil aviation is yet another arena in which China has assumed a more prominent role. Direct flights link Beijing to cities throughout the Northern Hemisphere: Chicago, Detroit, London, Frankfurt, Paris, Zurich, and Singapore. China participates in the International Civil Aviation Organization, which requires its members to file accident reports. In addition, three of China's airlines are members of the International Air Transport Association, which provides technical and managerial training. On the bilateral front, the United States and China have signed several agreements to share technical information on air traffic control and safety.

China's energy development is not subject to the rules of a single formal regime. The International Atomic Energy Agency, the World Bank, and APEC all influence the course of Chinese energy development, and the WTO will. Such multinational corporations as Amoco, Exxon, ARCO, Statoil of Norway, Occidental, and the Japanese National Oil Company have played major roles in introducing Chinese leaders and bureaucrats to the norms of international petroleum development, and these norms have significantly affected Chinese behavior. In addition, China's rapidly increasing demand for energy to fuel its economic growth has led to substantial interaction with the international community; in the petroleum industry, by 1988 foreign investment accounted for more than 50 percent of the total capital construction investment. China also has been aggressive in pursuing World Bank funds for projects such as the Changchun coal mine in Shanxi Province, the development of the Sichuan natural gas fields, and a number of energy efficiency and energy pricing programs. China has subjected some of its power plants to the international financial market by listing them on the New York Stock Exchange.

The People's Republic has joined international regimes in the environmental sphere. Its participation began in 1972 with Premier Zhou Enlai's attendance at the United Nations Conference on the Human Environment in Stockholm. Since then, China has been active in international organizations, agreements, and negotiations such as the Montreal Protocol on Substances That Deplete the Ozone Layer, the Convention in Trade and Endangered Species, the Convention on Biodiversity, and the Framework Convention on Climate Change. Chinese participation in international environmental regimes also involves extensive interaction with multilateral lending institutions, such as the World Bank and the Asian Development Bank, and with bilateral assistance programs that support environmental protection activities.

Even on the most politically sensitive of issues, human rights, China has undertaken commitments and participated in several international activities. In 1979, it began attending meetings of the U.N. Human Rights Commission as an observer, and it joined the commission in 1982. It has acceded to nine human rights conventions, including ones on the prevention and punishment of genocide, the status of refugees, elimination of racial discrimination, suppression and punishment of apartheid, elimination of discrimination against women, prevention of torture and other cruel, inhuman, or degrading punishment, protection of the rights of children, and equal remuneration for men and women for equal work. China has also supported U.N. investigations into human rights violations in Afghanistan and Chile and denounced the human rights records of Israel, South Africa, Vietnam, and Afghanistan. Furthermore, it issued human rights white papers in 1991 and 1995, with Li Peng stating explicitly that China "believe[s] that the human rights and fundamental freedoms of all mankind should be respected everywhere.... China agrees that questions concerning human rights should be the subject of normal international relations."

Perhaps most important is the headway China has made in the security realm. The People's Republic now participates in a range of accords that condemn the proliferation of conventional arms and weapons of mass destruction. For example, it pledged adherence to the 1963 Limited Test Ban Treaty in 1986 and endorsed the Comprehensive Test Ban Treaty in 1996. It has also acceded to the Nuclear Nonproliferation Treaty, signed the chemical and biological weapons conventions, supported Strategic Arms Reduction Talks (START) and the Intermediate-Range Nuclear Force talks, and reached bilateral agreements with the United States to adhere to the guidelines of the Missile Technology Control Regime.

China has become a member of official and semi-official international, regional, and subregional security dialogues such as the ASEAN Regional Forum (ARF) and the Committee on Security Cooperation in the Asia-Pacific region. Its strategic planners now routinely participate in the activities of leading think tanks around the world, such as the Stockholm International Peace Research Institute and the International Institute for Strategic Studies in London. And its most senior leaders, including its top military officials, are constantly traveling abroad or receiving foreign leaders.

Domestic Institutional Reforms

Another indication of the seriousness of Chinese intent to participate fully in the international system is the creation of national domestic institutions, policy communities, and laws and regulations to attain its external objectives and commitments.[3] Observers who assert that China has undertaken economic reform without political reform ignore the major structural adjustments China has made at the national level to aid its involvement in world affairs.

The Ministry of Foreign Affairs (MFA) and the Ministry of Foreign Trade and Economic Cooperation (MOFTEC) have expanded their personnel and competencies to deal with added responsibilities. China's once skeletal staffs in New York, Geneva, and Washington have become large bureaucracies, and the foreign affairs bureaus of commissions and ministries in Beijing have gone from dealing primarily with liaison and protocol to negotiation and oversight. MOFTEC and the MFA were once dwarfed by the State Planning Commission, the State Capital Construction Commission, and the State Economic Commission. Today, symbolic of the change, the two ministries occupy new, modern buildings, as do the Customs Administration, the Bank of China, and the China International Trust and Investment Corporation (CITIC).

In the economic sphere, convergent with domestic trends, the government has restructured itself to attract foreign technology, capital, and trade. The institutional arrangements for implementing foreign trade, for example, differ markedly from those of 10 or 20 years ago.[4] Since 1978, China has installed an entirely new system to attract foreign direct investment, encompassing legislation on foreign investment, tax laws, special economic zones, foreign exchange markets, intellectual property laws, and customs laws. New institutions have arisen on the Chinese landscape, such as CITIC and similar organizations at the provincial level; copyright, trademark, and patent offices; and the stock exchanges in Shanghai and Shenzhen. To facilitate World Bank lending, the State Council established a special division in the Ministry of Finance—China is the only large borrower to designate such a special unit—staffed by personnel who have spent extended periods in Washington. Specially created banks, such as the China Investment Bank and the China World Bank, channel funds from the World Bank, the Asian Development Bank, and bilateral concessionary loans.[5] Two new banking laws approved in 1995, the Central Bank Law and the Commercial Bank Law, are intended to bring China closer to international banking practices.[6] China has configured itself in more subtle ways to meet international financial standards, in statistical reporting, accounting procedures, and bidding practices. Undergirding these institutional developments is the growing number of think tanks and policy research groups, which have been influential in the formulation of China's domestic and foreign economic policy.[7]

In the field of intellectual property, national patent, copyright, and trademark protection, agencies have been established and a legal framework enacted. Intellectual property rights tribunals are being created in the court system, and international agencies and foreign governments are assisting in the training of officials.[8]

In civil aviation, China has adopted laws and regulations that directly reflect the influence of the international community, especially the United States. For example, in 1993 China and the United States began an intensive effort to train Chinese aviation authorities. The U.S. Federal Aviation Administration has taught American safety techniques, and Chinese pilots have received instruction in English. China has even modeled its new civil aviation guidelines after U.S. regulations, and plans to conduct all air-to-ground communications in English by 1998.[9]

In telecommunications, too, complex bureaucratic change has taken place, centering on the Ministry of Post and Telecommunications but involving other manufacturing ministries and providers including the Ministry of Electronic Industries, the Ministry of Railways, the People's Liberation Army (PLA), and the Ministry of Radio, Television, and Motion Pictures. Indeed, no sector exhibits more vividly than telecommunications the intense bureaucratic politics that swirl around China's international engagement. Some ministries resist external involvement because of the losses they would incur, while others stand to benefit greatly.

Domestic laws and institutions have also been established to implement various environmental accords. Key is the gradual building and strengthening of the National Environmental Protection Agency, which began in 1974 and culminated in 1988 with independent, subministerial status for the agency.[10] By 1992—not only as a reflection of China's international ties but primarily because of its pressing domestic environmental agenda—200 research institutes employed some 20,000 scientists and technicians engaged in environmental research.[11] For each environmental treaty China has signed, the leadership has established a complex arrangement of institutions to ensure that all relevant agencies are involved in the decision-making and implementation processes. Finally, government-approved nongovernmental agencies have begun to form, with some external funding, and are cooperating with various foreign environmental nongovernmental organizations.

Even in human rights some adjustments have been made, although noticeably fewer than elsewhere. The most sensitive issues in this domain—such as dealings with high-profile figures like Wei Jingsheng, Fang Lizhi, and the Dalai Lama—have remained in the hands of the top leaders. The Information Office of the State Council has begun to issue official white papers on human rights, presumably after it has coordinated the draft with the relevant organs in the political-legal sphere. The Ministry of Foreign Affairs represents China on human rights issues at the United Nations.[12] While some responsibilities in the legal and judicial spheres have been reassigned—the Ministry of Justice has taken over labor camps from the Ministry of Public Security—this issue remains under the coordinated leadership of the political-legal system and the *kou*, or mouth, of the Chinese Communist Party (CCP).[13] Efforts have also been made to strengthen the formal legal system. Some say this amounts to the introduction of the rule of law; others claim it means rule by law.[14] Developments have included the 1994 adoptions of a Prison Law, Law on Judges, Police Law, Procuracy Law, and 1996 revision of the Criminal Procedure Law.[15] Lawyers are beginning to appear in China, the courts' role in handling disputes is expanding, and some training of judges has begun.[16] It is unclear, however, whether all this has much to do with China's entry into the world community or is intended to align China with international human rights standards.

In the security realm, a flock of foreign policy and national security research centers have appeared, most with links to the Ministry of Foreign Affairs, the armed forces, or the Ministry of State Security (formerly the Communist Party's Department of Intelligence), or, in the Chinese fashion, patronized by a powerful leader.[17] Examples include the China Institute of Strategic Studies (formerly the Beijing Institute of Strategic Studies), the Shanghai Institute for International Relations, the Chinese Institute of Contemporary International Relations, the National Defense University, the new School of International Affairs at Beijing University, and the various regional centers' research institutes of the Chinese Academy of Social Sciences. Moreover, each foreign affairs agency has one or more research institutes, and the Foreign Affairs, State Security, and Foreign Trade and Economic Cooperation Ministries sponsor their own universities. Embedded in this constellation is an arms control community, many of whose members have received training in Geneva, the United States, and elsewhere; there are at least 280 specialists in China who have written on arms control issues in leading journals.[18]

Actual Behavior

In short, much has been accomplished in 25 years. China and the outside world—including the United States—have done a great deal to further their joint participation in international regimes. China's formal record of integration is extensive. It has reformed institutions to aid its participation in world affairs and allowed considerable external involvement in its development. To evaluate performance, however, one must go beyond the passage of laws, attendance at international meetings, and rhetoric aimed abroad to examine domestic policies, international behavior, and implementation at local levels. Here the record is decidedly more mixed.

Chinese behavior, our study group concluded, falls into seven categories: protecting sovereignty; maintaining security; eroding Taiwan's status; cultivating a favorable image; promoting economic interests; defending domestic political interests; and responding to regime characteristics. Several categories of behavior, including an often rigid insistence on protecting Chinese sovereignty, laying claim to Taiwan, and precluding Taiwan's independence have generally constrained China's participation in the world community. Others, such as the cultivation of a favorable image, have fostered participation. Still others, such as the use of foreign investment to enhance economic growth while protecting the domestic economy or to serve domestic political purposes, sometimes prohibit and sometimes encourage Chinese integration with the world.

Protecting Chinese Sovereignty

In their rhetoric, China's leaders have adopted the Western concept of sovereignty as a sacred principle. Defense of territorial integrity and national independence has become their rallying cry, and they use it to advance their own political interests. Chinese policies in the human rights and telecommunications regimes, for example, have reflected Chinese leaders' resolve to guard against the influx of foreign values and ideas, "to take what is 'good' from the outside world, and filter out what is potentially harmful to them."[19]

In the realm of human rights, although Beijing has occasionally adjusted its internal policies in response to external demands since 1978, in general it has defied the efforts of international human rights organizations and individual governments—especially the U.S. government—to judge China's performance and impose international standards on its political system. Beijing has imprisoned or forced into internal exile Chinese citizens who have sought to do so.

According to such evaluations, China remains a gross violator of basic civil and political human rights. Human rights specialists distinguish among three types of violations: 1) those that clearly transgress China's international obligations, defy its domestic law, and are indefensible even if one accepts extreme cultural relativism in standards; 2) those that contravene international standards and Chinese written law but that the outside world has largely ignored and even abetted through inaction and passivity; and 3) actions that seem repugnant to many both in China and abroad but are not universally accepted as violations of human rights (for example, the high-pressure family planning program and the export of goods produced by prison labor). Violations in the first category include imprisonment, arbitrary detention, and exile of people for their political beliefs; failure to abide by internationally recognized standards for criminal procedures, as in cases of torture, unlimited detention, arbitrary sentencing procedures, and faulty trial procedures; mistreatment of prisoners; and political intervention in the application of death sentences.[20] Violations in the second category include constraints on freedom of religion and the press; discrimination against ethnic minorities; surveillance of politically suspect citizens to the point of intimidation; forced abortions and sterilization; and severe constraints on the formation of voluntary organizations, especially free trade unions.

Despite China's lack of cooperation with international human rights organizations and its behavioral inadequacies, China's declared policy has increasingly conformed with international standards.[21] Moreover, the Chinese government has undertaken measures to address some of these inadequacies, such as the 1995 Judges Law and the 1996 amendments to the 1979 Criminal Procedures Law, although these have not ended the abuses.[22] Further, since 1989 the populace has enjoyed greater cultural latitude (though still constrained), greater geographical mobility, and greater choice in occupation, avocation, and lifestyle. Although government corruption is increasing and abuse of power is widespread, most Chinese probably enjoy more freedom today than at any point in recent history. However, since 1994, possibly because of the United States' abandonment of the linkage between trade and human rights, China's oppression of political dissidents has increased.

When a broad definition of human rights is employed to judge conformity with international standards, China ranks higher among nations. In many economic and social areas, Chinese behavior surpasses—often far surpasses—that of many other countries, although in areas such as health care, education, alleviation of poverty, and equitable distribution of income, the situation is worse than officially portrayed, and in other areas, such as income distribution and health care, past gains are eroding. Human rights activists stress, however, that China's commendable record on infant mortality rates and reduction of malnutrition does not compensate for abuses of basic civil rights.

In telecommunications, China has tried, with limited success, to control the types of technology introduced in the country, as well as their rate of introduction. Since 1989 the authorities have issued a series of decrees attempting to limit popular access to direct satellite television broadcasts. Sporadic enforcement of the decrees, however, especially outside the major cities, has sharply curtailed their impact.[23] The advent of the Internet in China has proved especially nettlesome. While leaders are eager to tap into the economic potential of the Internet, many are concerned about its potential for political subversion. By September 1996 the government had "blocked access from China to more than 100 Web sites deemed obscene or politically dangerous," including those for the *Wall Street Journal* and the *Washington Post.*[24] The government's decision to grant Xinhua News Service sole control over the distribution of foreign financial news—an effort unlikely to succeed in the long run—is also in part a reflection of political concerns.

China has been concerned to protect its sovereignty in the environmental realm as well, typically rejecting monitoring and reporting demands on environmental accords and refusing any agreement that might require transferring decision-making authority over natural resource management to an international body. Before the 1992 U.N. Conference on Environment and Development, Chinese negotiators tried hard to prevent a climate change agreement that would constrain the PRC's economic development in the short term by limiting coal usage or requiring the implementation of costly energy-efficient technologies. Notably, they set out five principles of negotiation that stressed China's right to control consumption of its natural resources.

Maintaining Chinese Security

The emphasis on sovereignty also shapes China's participation in the global security regime. China pursues "basically a state-centered, balance-of-power calculus intended to maintain China's strategic independence, rather than manifesting any deep concern for strengthening mutual security."[25] Beijing has been reluctant to endorse cooperative concepts of security and to accept the need to place real restrictions on Chinese military capabilities.

China's greatly expanded participation in arms control has primarily sought to protect and strengthen its strategic independence in the international arena. Conventional weapons acquisitions, which increase force projection capabilities, and advocacy by some nuclear strategists in leading think tanks urging China's development of nuclear weapons to deter or defeat strong conventional forces amassed on its periphery (a doctrine of limited deterrence) have implications for arms purchases and deployments by China's neighbors that could complicate current and future arms control efforts.[26]

Many Chinese strategic thinkers reject the notion that global interests have replaced national interests. "States with technological disadvantages," they assert, "will advocate arms control to restrict the state with the advantage."[27] Thus, they say, China should enter into arms control agreements that either restrict the technologically advanced states more than China or offer China an advantage vis-à-vis its militarily less developed neighbors. Not surprisingly, their logic lends particular support to measures that reduce the capabilities of others more than they do China's and avoid or delay implementation of measures that would reduce Chinese capabilities. China backs measures that cost it little and enhance its image. In sum, China's growing involvement in arms control negotiations has primarily taught it to use the arms control arena more effectively for its state-centric security purposes rather than prompting a reconsideration of how best to attain security.

Precluding Taiwan's Independence: Eroding Taiwan's Status

Attempts to erode Taiwan's international status and constrain its international activities are a third category of Chinese behavior in international regimes. The PRC expends significant diplomatic energy countering Taiwan's efforts to enhance its international status by gaining entry into international organizations or participating in international accords. Moreover, the PRC insists on setting the terms under which Taiwan is granted entry. For example, it has stipulated that Taiwan can only enter the WTO after the PRC has become a member. In addition, Taiwan has become a contentious issue in China's dealings with other nations, primarily in bilateral but occasionally in multilateral forums. Most recently, China threatened to veto a U.N. peace mission to Guatemala because Guatemala has formal diplomatic ties with Taiwan. In the end, the probable repercussions of the threatened veto for China's image in the U.N. General Assembly outweighed Chinese leaders' desire to punish Guatemala. Taiwan, however, remains an extremely sensitive issue in China's relations with the rest of the world.

Securing a Favorable International Image

Especially in the U.N. General Assembly, China shows considerable concern for its image—particularly among the less developed countries, of which it considers itself a leader. China relinquished some of its claim on International Development Agency loans so as to leave more money for loans to disaster-stricken Africa, thereby both making itself look good in the developing countries and demonstrating a commitment to internationalist values.[28] Its decision to accede to the Comprehensive Test Ban Treaty resulted in large measure from pressure from the developing world.

In arms control, China has balanced its reluctance to endorse cooperative concepts of security with its attempts to cultivate an international image as a champion of peace that does not seek to be a hegemonic power in Asia and, moreover, advocates complete disarmament. China wants to keep up the appearance of adhering to the pro-peace norms that a majority of nations support.[29] Its involvement in international arms control regimes continues to expand, and the cost of retreat or withdrawal increases proportionately, especially given growing international sentiment for arms control.[30] China has helped ensure the indefinite and unconditional extension of the Nuclear Nonproliferation Treaty and has supported the Comprehensive Test Ban Treaty. Furthermore, its activities in the diverse arms control forums have increased and only become significant in the last five years.[31] In addition, China has advanced some arms control proposals of its own, such as a convention on total elimination of nuclear weapons and a treaty pledging the five declared nuclear powers to "no first use."[32]

Concerns over its image have also led the PRC to pursue a mix of policies in the human rights arena. Its response to the widespread criticism in international forums of its human rights practices has combined ideological resistance and selective substantive concessions to rally Third World support, especially in multilateral settings; to appeal to advocates of realpolitik in the West; and to construct policy dilemmas for human right advocates.[33] Thus, while rhetorically and diplomatically rejecting interference on human rights, the government, since 1989, has offered a series of measured concessions combined with occasional, selective use of hardline tactics.[34] As with other areas of foreign policy, "China has made concessions it perceived as necessary to influence states with which it was interacting, and not [made] them when they were seen as not necessary."[35]

Promoting Economic Development and Protecting Domestic Procedures

Chinese involvement in trade and financial regimes promotes its economic development and social stability, but increasingly the leaders have constrained further integration because of the risks. Participation in these regimes has contributed substantially to China's economic growth; at the same time, it necessitates opening borders and exposing Chinese firms to foreign competition. In a number of instances, China has elected to limit the extent to which it exposes its industries to outside competition. China's participation in the regimes governing trade and investment, banking and finance, telecommunications, and the environment all entail balancing promotion of economic growth with protection of domestic producers.

During the last several years, China's participation in formal regimes such as Intellectual Property Rights (IPR) and efforts to accede to the WTO have been marked by domestic controversy, while individual business transactions have skyrocketed. Regimes such as WTO and IPR involve substantial institutional intertwining between China and the outside world and necessitate a willingness by at least one party to absorb high short-term costs in pursuit of long-term gains.[36] Conflicts naturally erupt between China and other major actors, especially the United States but including Japan and the European Union, over the allocation of these costs. Even if China gains membership in the WTO this year, trade disputes are likely to persist, as China's export surge almost surely will continue.

An export-oriented sector has taken root under the sponsorship of Taiwanese, Hong Kong, South Korean, and Japanese manufacturers: "The strongest growth in exports has been achieved by foreign funded enterprises and PRC firms engaged in export processing."[37] Fully 60 percent of growth in exports from 1985 to 1994 is attributable to foreign-funded enterprises.[38] Nonetheless, China's demand for capital goods in the telecommunications, transportation, electronics, energy, and petrochemical sectors as well as its imports of agricultural products, petroleum, and high-quality steel will preclude China from having overall trade surpluses.

China simultaneously exhibits strong protectionist impulses. The state-owned enterprises, which still constitute a large portion of heavy industry, produce a declining share of China's exports. These enterprises remain heavily protected by nontariff barriers, although tariffs are being reduced. Thus the core of the Chinese economy remains rather insulated from the competitive pressures of the world economy.

Moreover, since 1994 and in the Ninth Five Year Plan, China's top leaders officially adopted an industrial policy to protect fledgling industries. The list of these pillar industries has fluctuated, at various times including electronics, construction materials, telecommunications, automobiles, and aircraft. The rationale is understandable: to protect new industries that will have a large domestic market or have security implications. The State Planning Commission and the production ministries are the strongest proponents of this policy, even as they recognize that it has greatly complicated China's bid to enter the WTO. MOFTEC officials have indicated that production ministries believe that as long as China is not a member of the WTO, they do not need to consider WTO rules. Other, related manifestations of continued Chinese protectionism include various barriers to market access, a reluctance to grant national treatment to foreign enterprises in China, and persistent difficulties in implementing legislation on intellectual property rights.[39]

Protectionist impulses are also evident in the banking and finance sectors. The Chinese are still not fully prepared to meet international equity markets' demands for competitive rates of return for foreign lenders to development projects. In its move to join the international financial system, China is most recalcitrant about a full opening to banking services and insurance and financial services (for instance, permitting foreign firms into the credit card business or allowing them to have seats on Chinese stock exchanges and to participate in all share transactions). Beijing has taken tentative steps in all these areas, but the barriers remain high, as China's domestic institutions would be vulnerable to the competition. Reform of domestic banking, related to the successful transformation of inefficient state-owned enterprises to which banks have extended sizable nonperforming loans, is essential to complete China's integration into the international financial system. And the leadership has continually postponed such reform, concerned about the consequent economic and possible social instability that would arise.[40]

Economic interests also have constrained China's integration into the global telecommunications system. While the International Telecommunication Union's advocacy of interoperable communications technologies has helped foreign companies gain access to the Chinese market, the Chinese have resisted the wholesale import of foreign technologies and set restrictions on levels of direct foreign investment. Nonetheless, foreign investors, especially overseas Chinese, have been eating away at the relatively restrictive foreign investment policies of the PRC.[41]

Even in the realm of civil aviation, there are allegations that Chinese authorities are trying to limit the access of foreign airlines to the Chinese market. For example, Chinese officials reportedly pressure companies to use Chinese-owned cargo airlines and passengers to use Chinese carriers for their travel.

At the same time, leaders recognize that continued economic growth and participation in global markets will require China to adapt its institutions and policies to the demands of the market. In this sense, the market has served as an enforcer of reform. For example, in banking, the protectionist leanings have been balanced by an equally significant effort to comply with the standards of international capital markets. Of particular note, China has exposed itself to the rigors of international financial markets, testing its creditworthiness, subjecting itself to Standard and Poor's and Moody's investment ratings, and withdrawing offerings when the market judged their risk high and therefore demanded higher interest payments. Rather than condemning the judgment as a capitalist conspiracy, the Chinese have begun to take some compensatory measures, and the risk factor has begun to be reduced. Chinese behavior in the international financial system, for example, has been greatly influenced by the necessity of conforming to market forces. World Bank lending to China has increased rapidly because of the country's excellent record with the bank's loans. Bank officials consider China's record as exemplary, certainly in comparison to India.[42]

Chinese behavior in the energy sector further confirms the market's importance as a natural enforcer of reform. China's continued economic development hinges on its ability to secure ever greater amounts of energy. Thus the energy sector has become increasingly open to foreign involvement. China now depends heavily on the international community for assistance in developing its oil and gas reserves as well as its electric power capacity. In addition, Beijing has responded directly to international demands for change. Under pressure from the multilateral banks, China has opened its doors to competitive bidding and begun some price reforms. In addition, in the oil industry, economic interests and the need for technical expertise have gradually come to outweigh national security concerns and the desire to protect domestic industry.[43] Overall, the energy sectors that have experienced the most reform—petroleum and electric power—have been the ones most affected by international markets.[44]

China's involvement in the international civil aviation regime also suggests that market interests have encouraged the country to accommodate itself to the norms that govern the international economy. China's actions are driven in substantial measure by the rapid expansion of its internal aviation market and its desire to secure access to foreign markets, as well as ensure adequate air safety. Although the nations of the Asia-Pacific region are engaged in a nascent effort to establish a regional approach to aviation policy—one potential result would be a "bamboo curtain" in which Asia would act as a bloc against U.S. interests—given the Chinese desire to gain access to lucrative markets abroad, such as that of the United States, the PRC may well reject such a regional effort.[45]

Advancing Domestic Political Interests

Chinese participation in international affairs is an extension of its domestic politics. When the leaders derive more benefits than participation costs them, they will involve themselves in a regime. These benefits include enhanced domestic status, financial resources, or useful ideas and information. But when the costs exceed the benefits, they will not cooperate. Chinese participation, in short, is driven by a domestic cost-benefits analysis. For example, the benefits the leaders obtain from World Bank membership far outweigh the costs: first and foremost, they receive funds that they can disburse among ministries and provinces. But membership in the WTO is something else: China's compliance with WTO standards will have to be exacted from ministries and provinces, with no immediate and discernible payoffs for the leadership.

The degree of consensus in the uppermost echelons of government also affects China's entry. If there is a strong consensus among the top leaders that integration meets China's interests, or if a single leader attaches importance to an otherwise lower priority issue and energizes the effort, entry might go forward. The opposite is also true: no support at the top means a greatly reduced chance of participation.

In each realm, many officials support deeper integration. They believe China would benefit greatly from full participation in this regime; they are confident that China would acquit itself well and become a leader in that area. Even on human rights, there are advocates of more humane and responsive rule. At the same time, each area has its vociferous opponents of integration or deep integration. One senses beneath the surface an ongoing struggle between the proponents and opponents of further integration, and Chinese behavior reflects the current balance between the contending forces.

Moreover, participation in an international regime ultimately is in the hands of Chinese bureaucracies. But usually their domestic missions are more important than their international responsibilities, and their domestic missions shape the response to the international involvement. China's coercive bureaucracies—the PLA, the Ministry for State Security, and the Ministry of Public Security—are at the core of China's domestic and external security systems, and naturally they bring a security perspective to issues of arms control and human rights. The economic bureaucracies—the State Planning Commission, the People's Bank, MOFTEC, the Bank of China, and MOF (Ministry of Finance)—bring to bear a different set of considerations, which are tied to maximizing China's growth rate while balancing unemployment and inflation. They must coordinate integration into the financial and trade regimes while managing the economy. The Ministry of Foreign Affairs has a clear mandate to introduce Taiwan and other sovereignty issues into the calculus.

To understand China's policies, one must understand the bureaucratic politics and interests at work. As in the United States, most foreign policies involve several agencies and require coordination among often competing agencies. When the bureaucratic interests of China's participating agencies diverge, the likelihood increases that participation will lack coherence, consistency, and continuity. For example, with respect to conventional arms sales, China will say one thing and do another because those who enunciate policy do not control the vendors: the two live in different parts of the system. Other examples are intellectual property rights and telecommunications, where the competing interests simply cannot be easily reconciled.[46]

China's efforts to meet its energy needs through cooperation with the international community also are constrained by both national security concerns and institutional inefficiencies. Chinese institutions are reluctant to pay for foreign personnel and experts; state-owned enterprises often refuse to yield management control over assets and personnel;[47] foreign enterprises cannot hold majority stakes; the natural gas pricing system has not been fully reformed; and the coal industry presents problems due to a "lack of management, ownership, pricing and legal reforms."[48]

When a single agency is responsible for formulating policy, establishing the institutional framework to implement the policy, and then enforcing the policy, the likelihood of coherence and consistency is greater. China's policy on nuclear testing is an example; the people who commit China to cease nuclear tests are the same ones who give the order to test.

Chinese behavior also reflects the responsible agencies' capacity to implement policy, especially their financial resources, quality of personnel, legal context, and the priority attached to the issue at lower levels.[49] The weaker the capacity, the weaker the compliance with international commitments. Environment is an excellent example. Institutional weakness in the banking sphere precludes a policy of deep financial integration because of concern about the consequences. However, in the telecommunications sphere, the regime's limited capacity to enforce the ban on satellite dishes actually furthers integration.

Responding to Regime Characteristics

Finally, Chinese behavior responds to and takes advantage of the nature of the international regime: its governance, the degree of international consensus over its norms, and the regime's trajectory.

- *The type of regime.* China responds more favorably to impersonal and market regimes, where the rules of the game apply equally to all countries. The international financial regime is a case in point. Regimes organized and led by the industrial democracies for their benefit or enforced primarily by the United States are more likely to be resisted.
- *The degree of international consensus about the regime.* Some regimes

are characterized by a high degree of consensus about their norms, while others are in considerable dispute. China finds it easier to enter regimes that lack a consensus. In such cases, it can choose the norms to which it will adhere. But the lack of consensus renders China's participation less meaningful. Its range of choice, along with that of other members of the regime, has not been narrowed. Obviously, its latitude is limited when a regime enjoys a consensus about its norms. China does join such regimes, but it is more likely thereafter to complain that the rules were formed without it. Its degree of actual compliance, then, depends on the cost-benefit calculus. Ambiguities in the human rights and intellectual property rights regimes, for example, give China the opportunity to maneuver and manipulate, while the financial regime imposes strict standards.

- *The evolution of the regime.* International regimes themselves undergo change. For example, World Bank lending priorities change. The environmental and telecommunications sectors feel this especially strongly, but changes are also occurring in the arms control area, human rights, and so on. Change presents China with both opportunity and challenge. The opportunity is to help shape the nature of the change; the challenge is to accept the responsibility to participate in the setting of the rules. In several instances, by the time China has equipped itself to enter a regime and support its purposes, the regime has transformed itself. For example, the International Tropical Timber Agreement was established to govern trade in tropical timber but by the late 1980s had developed a secondary focus on the protection of tropical timber. Still, in China, the ministry with primary responsibility for that agreement is the Ministry of Foreign Trade and Economic Cooperation, which has stymied participation by the now more relevant Ministry of Forestry. China participates most effectively in regimes whose trajectories converge with the path that China is pursuing because of its own domestic considerations.

Impact on Regimes

On the whole, China has been passive in the regimes it has joined. Only in the environmental and human rights spheres has China actively sought to shape the norms of the regime; in both instances, its efforts collide with the American position. But even in those important areas, China has made its case within the regime rather than outside it. It has not sought to create alternative regimes under its control, as the Soviet Union did in the organization of the Warsaw Pact, the Communist International, and the Soviet-led trade bloc. Most vexing is its possible dissemination of weapons and technologies of mass destruction, where its behavior matches the dubious and disturbing record of several other major powers.

Proof of China's minimal impact on the regimes is clear in the United Nations. The United Nations' importance for China's quest for legitimacy as a great power remains undiminished in the post-Tiananmen and post-Cold War years. China's veto in the U.N. Security Council ensures its status and safeguards its sovereignty. For the most part, China has behaved as a status quo power in the United Nations, not a reformer or system-transforming revolutionary. It plays by the established rules rather than attempting to replace or repudiate them.[50]

Neither the worst fears of a disruptive China in the U.N. system nor the best hopes of a constructively and extensively involved China have been realized. Without China's participation, the regimes would not be truly international. China's sheer presence bestows legitimacy on the regime. And on balance, its conduct has alleviated tensions between the developing and the developed world.

Interviews with numerous U.N. diplomats around the world yielded a surprising degree of consensus concerning the nature of China's participation in the Security Council and General Assembly. One delegate observed, "When I first arrived at the United Nations, I expected the Chinese to have a very high profile, particularly among developing countries. I was startled to find that the general opinion of the Chinese was very low among these countries, including the Asian countries."[51] Another representative summarized the Chinese posture this way: "How do you imagine you could ever force the Chinese to do anything? Nothing can be done against the Chinese. . . . They believe in bilateral dealing. They come. They smile. They leave."[52]

The interviews suggest that a low level of engagement best characterizes Chinese involvement on most issues. China is almost becoming a "group of one [G-1]." According to a European diplomat, "The Chinese are not interested anymore. They are feeling less and less in common with the Permanent Five. They don't feel they should have to sacrifice their independence because they are a P5 member, and they feel they stand to lose more by identifying with the P5 than by allying themselves with the Nonaligned Movement. They don't feel a need to contribute constructively." A Latin American diplomat concurred: "They never take part in the give and take of preparing resolutions. . . . If they can, they let others weave together a resolution, then say they can live with it. They do not waste any time on things that are not fundamental to their interests."

U.N. agencies such as the U.N. Educational, Social, and Cultural Organization (UNESCO), the International Children's Emergency Fund (UNICEF), the Development Program (UNDP), and the Food and Agriculture Organization (FAO) are very active in China, where they enjoy excellent relations with Beijing. Moreover, despite some contentious encounters in the U.N. arms control and disarmament and human rights regimes, China, unlike the United States, has yet to withdraw from any international regime, and it pays its dues on time. Chinese behavior in the Security Council and the General Assembly is best characterized as passive, occasionally obstreperous, with a tendency to acquiesce to U.N.

actions rather than actively support or oppose them. Abstention after drawing attention to itself through delaying tactics is the preferred Chinese position on controversial issues brought before the Security Council. This posture can be interpreted as free-riding, reaping the benefits from the U.N. action against Iraq, for example, while bearing none of the costs. China extracts a price from the industrial democracies by forbearing to exercise its veto, and enhances its stature among other countries by expressing reservations about an action. On the other hand, China's passive posture can be seen as a blessing in disguise. China's voting record in the General Assembly places it among those countries most often opposed to the U.S. position. If China were more active in the United Nations, like the Soviet Union in the heyday of the Cold War, the United States might find itself in a more difficult position. China has chosen not to turn the United Nations into an arena of diplomatic conflict.

CHINESE OBJECTIVES, CAPABILITIES, AND STRATEGIES IN WORLD AFFAIRS

Chinese participation in international regimes over the past two decades provides further insight into China's broader foreign policy objectives, capabilities, and strategies.[53]

Objectives and Perceptions

China's leaders, like those of most countries, pursue four major objectives in their dealings with the outside world. They strive to attain national security, maintain national unity, and protect the sovereignty of their country. They wish to obtain access to foreign markets and to secure technology, natural resources, and capital to stimulate economic development. They want to have a voice in the councils of nations that satisfies their sense of dignity and permits them to influence decisions that affect their country's fate. Finally, they seek to use the international arena to enhance their domestic power, political stature, and possibly their familys' fortunes.

Different leaders, bureaucracies, and regions weigh these objectives differently. Some assign higher priority to pursuit of policies that yield maximum growth for the economy, while others are more concerned with security or domestic stature. Many citizens resent the corruption accompanying China's involvement in world affairs and the privileges the elite have secured through their foreign connections. Nonetheless, the leaders and the people are united in their view of modern Chinese history. All believe that their country was exploited and humiliated by outside aggressors, when their weak predecessors were forced to cede Chinese territory, and that vigilance is now required to protect China's sovereignty. They also tend to believe that China's stability is fragile; any domestic or foreign policy is evaluated, in part, on its consequences for China's unity.

Leaders are also driven by deep-seated fears of resurgent Japanese militarism, future Russian expansionism, U.S. resistance to China's rise and an American missionary impulse to press foreign values on the country, Indian desire to dominate the South Asian subcontinent and perhaps to emerge as a rival to China, and, more recently, a Taiwanese drift toward independence or a return to the Japanese security orbit. These concerns, informed by the history of the last 200 years, prompt wariness toward existing international arrangements that have been formulated by one or more of the major powers. China's leaders harbor suspicions that these arrangements, peddled as serving the common interest of all humanity, were devised primarily by dominant powers to advance their own interests. In the security sphere, the rulers in Beijing tend to approach the very notions of building international norms and creating international regimes with deep distrust, believing these are the disguised efforts of the dominant powers that formulated them to bind weaker powers into systems that perpetuate the current global distribution of power and wealth.

Linked to this view are other widespread conceptions about international affairs—namely, that governments are the dominant actors, there is an inevitable hierarchy among nations, international relations are a zero-sum game, and international affairs involve great fluidity as the capacities of nations continually wax and wane. Hence, security does not turn on interdependence. China can attain security through intimidation and the arousal of limited fear in its partners. Thus the leaders of China are tough-minded, practical, realistic, and unsentimental practitioners of statecraft; they would not have survived and mounted the ladder of Chinese domestic politics otherwise. Although they have no use for sentiment, they expect foreign leaders to treat them with respect and they exhibit great emotion over issues they believe intrude on China's sovereignty. They tend to seek greater deference than they are prepared to bestow on others. Claiming to offer friendship and certainly capable of great hospitality to foreigners, most Chinese leaders nonetheless remain aloof and remote. These deep-seated attitudes and traits do not make them easy partners in world affairs.

Capabilities

The leaders of China derive influence from the sheer size of their land and its population, expectations of China's future greatness, and their capacity to affect regional balances of power in Northeast Asia, Southeast Asia, South Asia, and Central Asia. China's location places its leaders at the hub of a vast region stretching from Japan to Pakistan, home to over three billion people and the world's most dynamic economies. China's membership in the club of states with nuclear weapons and its permanent membership on the U.N. Security Council give its rulers added influence. The leaders command international status as representatives of a great civilization and a talented populace.

And in the last 15 years, China's leaders have gained an enhanced voice in world affairs through their nation's economic performance. China now has over $100 billion in foreign currency reserves, second in the world. It has jumped to 11th place in total world trade, and its economy clearly ranks among the four largest in the world—the exact position depending on the criteria used in evaluation.

Moreover, in the last 20 years, China's leaders have attained numerous foreign policy objectives. They agreed to establish diplomatic relations with the United States only when Washington severed its formal relations with the Republic of China on Taiwan, including its defense treaty with the island. Sino-Soviet relations improved only as the Kremlin—first under Mikhail Gorbachev, then Boris Yeltsin—essentially met the conditions Deng Xiaoping had specified. Sino-Vietnamese relations improved only after Vietnam withdrew its forces from Cambodia (Kampuchea) and Hanoi abandoned its dream of dominating the Indochina peninsula. China improved relations with India while maintaining a strategic relationship with Pakistan and sustaining a de facto, peaceful boundary with New Delhi along Beijing's preferred demarcation. Hong Kong will return to the Chinese fold essentially on the terms Deng outlined. The People's Republic has developed an extensive and beneficial relationship with Taiwan without sacrificing its territorial claims on the island. After an interval of distancing itself following the government's June 4, 1989, repression of the prodemocracy demonstrators in Beijing, the outside world was back on China's doorstep. To be sure, China showed flexibility and made significant compromises in attaining all these objectives, and Beijing continues to pay for its brutal handling of the 1989 demonstrations.

Yet several important objectives have not been attained. Relations with the United States have become somewhat strained. The ASEAN states are coalescing, partly out of concern over China's growing strength, and Vietnam has joined their orbit. The goals of achieving Taiwan's reunification with the mainland and constraining South Korean and Japanese latitude in foreign policy remain elusive. In China's key northeast Asian backyard, it could be argued, Japan, South Korea, and Taiwan have acquired at least as much leverage over China as Beijing has gained over them. Nevertheless, this may be the most secure and tranquil environment China has enjoyed since the Opium War of 1839–42.

Deng Xiaoping and his colleagues attained their goals with a country that is not powerful by ordinary measures of national capability. China is a classic case of an influential but not powerful country. It lacks the ability to project military might beyond its borders for sustained periods, and estimates of its military might two or three decades hence suggest it will still be militarily vulnerable.[54] Indeed, U.S. government estimates of defense spending in East Asia reveal that China's expenditures have been steadily declining as a percentage of the total for the region. (See the table on page 35.)

To be sure, China possesses missiles armed with nuclear warheads, and it has amply demonstrated its willingness to use force in pursuit of foreign policy objectives. These characteristics distinguish it from most of its East and Southeast Asian neighbors. Nonetheless, China's defense expenditures relative to those of its immediate neighbors peaked in the 1970s. While Chinese capabilities have steadily improved, so have those of Japan, Korea, Taiwan, and the ASEAN states. Moreover, although China is spending more on defense compared to Russia and the United States than a decade ago, Washington and Moscow are still in a different league in terms of strategic capability. In short, China is not a military colossus among pygmies. And if it threatens to seek military dominance in the region, it could easily provoke a coalescence of force opposing it.

ASIAN GOVERNMENTS' MILITARY EXPENDITURES

(1994 constant U.S. $)

	1970		1975		1980		1985		1990		1994*	
	$million	% of Asia	$million	% of Asia	$million	% of Asia	$million	% of Asia	$million	% of Asia	$million	% of Asia
China	56, 680	65%	55, 645	54%	56, 193	48%	53, 235	41%	52, 611	36%	52, 800	34%
Japan	14, 506	17%	20, 788	20%	26, 948	23%	34, 018	26%	42, 507	29%	45, 800	29%
South Korea	1, 393	2%	2, 580	2%	6, 778	6%	8, 224	6%	11, 344	8%	13, 000	8%
Taiwan	3, 599	4%	3, 746	4%	5, 583	5%	8, 537	7%	10, 016	7%	11, 500	7%
North Korea	2, 067	2%	9, 317	9%	7, 697	7%	7, 024	5%	6, 611	5%	5, 500	3%
Southeast Asia	4, 865	6%	6, 792	7%	9, 018	8%	9, 718	7%	12, 052	8%	16, 089	10%
South Asia	3, 980	5%	4, 909	5%	6, 083	5%	9, 064	7%	10, 698	7%	12, 500	8%
TOTAL ASIA	87, 090		103, 777		118, 300		129, 820		145, 839		157, 300	
% OF WORLD	10%		10%		11%		10%		12%		19%	
WORLD	885, 600		992, 500		1, 089, 000		1, 272, 000		1, 203, 000		840, 300	

*All 1994 figures are estimates.
Source: US Arms Control and Disarmament Agency

Economically, too, China is less powerful than the aggregate figures suggest. The economy continues to be plagued by several serious problems. The central government's ability to mobilize revenue and control foreign trade is limited, and per capita income remains low. The coastal regions have sustained high growth through an export-led strategy that leaves the central government vulnerable to some extent to foreign and domestic pressures. Moreover, the accumulation of large foreign currency reserves and foreign indebtedness give China a stake in maintaining the current international financial system and encourage responsible behavior. As other nations have discovered, expanded involvement in the international economy does not easily translate into increased power.

In the realm of ideas, China now imports far more than it exports. It is a borrower of foreign technologies on an enormous scale. Visions of a modern China a generation down the road come largely from abroad, supplied by overseas Chinese, the "Asian tigers," and the West. China's youth are influenced by the teenage culture of the outside world. The Chinese government's protracted neglect of its educational system, its stifling of intellectual creativity, and its attack on its rich cultural heritage during the Maoist era have all taken their toll. Its former state ideology, Marxism-Leninism, no longer appears to offer great insight into the modernization process or assists leaders in prescribing policy. Nor can Deng's successors claim a mandate to rule that strong leaders gain through war, revolution, resolution of a crisis, or the ballot box. The successors to the revolutionary generation have not yet enunciated an ideology that could galvanize the nation behind them, although some form of nationalism may help perform that feat.

Thus China's ascent in coming decades is by no means assured or inevitable, and in any case is likely to be a protracted process. There is a discrepancy between the actual power of China's leaders and the image of their power. They possess less power both than they wish to have and than many foreign leaders and observers attribute to them. They may also be somewhat less powerful than they judge themselves to be. These gaps partially explain many aspects of Chinese external behavior both in bilateral relations and international regimes—for example, secrecy and bravado can shield leaders' sense of vulnerability. Their ambitious goals necessitate their immersion in world affairs. Their limited power requires them to be cautious so that others will not exploit their weaknesses.

Explaining Chinese Success

How can one reconcile China's effectiveness in attaining its foreign policy objectives with the weaknesses and vulnerabilities of its leaders? Four factors help explain the paradox. First, the outside world, especially the United States, learned between 1949 and 1971 the dangers and costs of isolating China. It seems better to forge good relations with China at an early stage in its possible rise than wait until Beijing has the power to force its way into international regimes. Second, China's internal reforms over the past 25 years have better equipped it to participate in world affairs. On balance, a reforming, opening, and economically developing China has served the interests of regional stability and global prosperity. Its altered posture has elicited a positive response from others. Third, China's many foreign policy successes flow from the resolute, disciplined behavior of its leaders and from the intelligent strategies they often pursued in world affairs, particularly at the height of the Deng Xiaoping era. These strategies are manifest in China's conduct in all the international regimes in which it participates.

Finally, ethnic Chinese in Hong Kong, Taiwan, Southeast Asia, and North America, as well as tens of thousands of recent émigrés from the People's Republic, have played a major role in accelerating China's entrance onto the world stage. They have been a source of capital, technology, and policy advice. They have channeled foreign influences into China, and with their knowledge of the outside world, have assisted in the expansion of the PRC's foreign involvement. They have had a moderating effect on China's international behavior, especially in the economic realm, where their contacts and influence are great, less so in the security realm, which is largely beyond their reach. In the realm of human rights, the message they deliver is ambiguous, with some championing the human rights agenda and others encouraging Beijing to reject foreign pressure.

Strategies of Participation

Beijing employs a distinctive array of interrelated strategies and tactics to advance its foreign policy objectives.[55] These strategies are manifest in both multilateral and bilateral relations:

- Play a balance-of-power role, tilting toward the side that most eagerly seeks an alignment with China. Thus Beijing leaned toward Moscow in the early 1950s when Stalin appreciated the added strength he gained from an alliance with China, and it cooperated with Washington in the orchestrated opposition to Soviet expansionism in the latter stages of the Cold War. Chinese diplomacy suffers when it lacks suitors.

- Steer between the major powers, seeking to exacerbate tensions between them, as a way of generating suitors. China is particularly sensitive to the dangers of condominium arrangements aimed against it, as with the Soviet Union and the United States in the 1960s and 1970s and with Japan and the United States in the 1990s.

- Retain flexibility in foreign policy conduct, avoid enduring commitments and entangling alignments. This strategy suggests that at least some Chinese leaders and strategists believe the only thing more harmful than exclusion from an international regime is binding and constraining inclusion in it.

- Demonstrate a credible resolve to employ military might in a carefully controlled fashion for limited objectives. Beijing has perfected the art of "coercive diplomacy," the pursuit of diplomacy against the background of a limited use of force. Recent examples include Chinese behavior in the South China Sea and toward Taiwan.

- Develop military might as economic conditions, available technology, and the international environment permit.

- Seek to use ethnic Chinese living outside mainland China as sources of influence abroad and sources of technology and capital for the People's Republic.

- Free-ride, seeking influence without shouldering responsibility, acquiescing to policies of international regimes that manifestly serve

China's interest while expressing reservations about the policies. Then extract side payments for acquiescence while whispering to the policies' opponents that the major powers pressured China to acquiesce. This strategy is quite evidently at work in China's behavior in the United Nations.

In pursuing the above strategies, China employs these tactics:

- State Chinese objectives clearly, succinctly, and repeatedly, and make compliance with these objectives the litmus test of whether the interlocutor wants "good" or "friendly" relations with China; place the burden of maintaining "good" relations on the other side.
- Mobilize support among developing countries for China's position.
- Play on ambiguities in the norms of international regimes.
- Adopt an aggrieved posture, capture the moral high ground, and put the interlocutor—whether a country, a regional organization, or an international regime—on the defensive, claiming it owes China special consideration because of past injustices.
- Trade on expectations of China's future greatness, asserting that those who favor China now and behave in a friendly fashion will be rewarded later.
- Employ access to the China market for maximum advantage; hold foreign firms hostage in attempts to influence their countries' foreign policy.
- Decry the effort of others to make cooperation with China in one substantive or geographic region conditional on progress in another (i.e., a "linkage" strategy), while at the same time pursuing a Chinese policy of linkage, threatening, for example, retaliation against Germany or Australia in the trade arena because of their welcome of the Dalai Lama and expressions of concern about Tibet, or implying that the American sale of F-16s to Taiwan helped prompt the transfer of advanced weapons to Pakistan.
- Maintain secrecy and opacity.

- Enter into agreements knowing China lacks the capacity to implement them not out of insincerity but as part of an effort to enmesh the outside party in a program to help China develop the necessary capability.

Changes in Chinese Foreign Policy

Although many of the broad objectives and strategies remain the same, Chinese foreign policy has changed somewhat since 1971. China's changing capabilities, the rise of new leaders, and a different strategic setting have had their effect.

The early days were characterized by a certain idealism—a desire for China to contribute positively to the regime involved—although the contribution the Chinese desired to make was on behalf of the developing world against the established order. Increasingly, engagement appears calculated more in terms of the short-term costs and benefits for China. Two examples capture the evolution. On joining the United Nations as a permanent member of the Security Council, China volunteered to increase its dues, from 4 percent to 5.5 percent of the total U.N. core budget. The request was unprecedented; no nation had ever sought to increase its payments to the United Nations. But in 1979 China asked for and was granted lower dues, 0.79 percent of the budget, in line with other developing countries. In the economic sphere, China in the early 1970s was an ardent supporter of the developing world and advocated major transformations of the international economy; it loomed as a potential threat to established telecommunications or financial regimes. Today it derives revenue from its participation in those regimes, and often seeks more.

In the early 1970s China adopted a low profile in the regimes that it joined. While its rhetoric was often ideological and strident, its behavior was disciplined and restrained; certainly this characterizes China's early behavior in the United Nations. Eager to join the regime, the Chinese were not overly concerned with the details of entry. But by the late 1980s and early 1990s the Chinese had become more assertive and tougher in their negotiation positions. For example, the Chinese delegation demanded major changes in the Montreal accords on protecting the earth's ozone layer before China would accede to the agreement. In such trade matters as intellectual property rights and entry into the WTO, Chinese negotiators have also proceeded from well-crafted positions that are intended to defend their country's economic interests. Retreat from initial bargaining positions in area after area has occurred only after considerable external pressure has been brought to bear.

Five factors help explain the evolution from idealism to practicality, from ideology to economic rationality, and from reticence to nationalistic assertiveness: generational change, a learning curve, evolution in the domestic policy process, an altered international environment, and Chinese economic success.

Generational Change

China's kaleidoscopic modern history has produced sharp differences among generations. Each generation endured distinctive traumas and socializing experiences in its formative years, such as the Japanese invasion (1931–45), the Great Leap Forward and the resulting famine (1957–62), and the disruptions of the Cultural Revolution (1966–76). These did not weld each generation into a cohesive whole; instead, every generation splintered over its members' diverse reactions to the defining trauma, and each group for its lifetime grappled with the distinctive issues the trauma posed. Those who matured in the 1920s and 1930s, deeply affected by nationalistic sentiment, wondered how best to cure China of its weakness and leave behind its inferior status, through ideologically militant defiance of the outside world or an idealistic effort to join and contribute to it. Those maturing in the Soviet era wrestled with their response to the Russian system: whether to conform to it or seek to change it. Those who survived the Cultural Revolution and prospered had learned to seize opportunities in an often bewildering environment.

The evolution in Chinese motivations for participating in international affairs partially reflects generational succession. In the 1970s, the formulation and implementation of policy lay with communist recruits of the 1920s to mid-1940s. They included ideologues and idealists, rustics from peasant backgrounds and urbane, well-educated Chinese who had been exposed to the West in their youth. That generation harbored ambivalent attitudes toward the West, but clearly relished the opportunity to play pivotal roles in the initial stages of China's reintegration into the world. By the mid-1980s, that generation was fading. Party recruits of the late 1940s and the 1950s who had risen in the post-1949 bureaucracy, many of them trained in the Soviet Union and Eastern Europe, were coming to the fore.

In the 1990s, the Cultural Revolutionaries, who are entrepreneurial, assertive, and often lack extensive formal education, have begun to make themselves felt. This generation clearly relishes the opportunity to calculate how China's rise can benefit them and their country. Many of its members appear eager to accelerate China's involvement in world affairs, but in an assertive and nationalistic way. Soon after them will come a very different cohort that matured in the Deng era, many among them with substantial experience in the West. On balance, this evolution in human talent is gradually equipping China for extensive involvement in world affairs, although at present there is a deficiency of qualified people that is partially remedied by ethnic Chinese from Taiwan, Hong Kong, and Southeast Asia.

Changes in the Policy Process

Early on in China's entry into the international community, the Chinese political system was highly centralized. Foreign policy was in the hands of a few people who brought discipline and coherence to the process. The subsequent expansion of China's involvement in world affairs, coupled with administrative decentralization, makes it impossible for a few people at the top to control foreign relations. While a handful of individuals can enforce their will on matters of highest priority to them, they cannot monitor every transaction that crosses the Chinese border, as was the case in the early 1970s. The ideological tone of China's early engagement reflected Mao's dominance of the system. The apparent pragmatism of the mid-1990s is a product of bureaucratic bargaining and a consultative, consensual policy process.

Moreover, the domestic budgetary system has changed. Every government unit and enterprise in China is under increasing budgetary pressure and has incentives to earn foreign currency and establish sources of domestic and foreign revenue. Local environmental agencies, for example, depend on the fines they collect from polluters to finance construction of their office buildings. Research centers use a substantial part of the per diem consulting charges billed to international funders to support their administrative staff. Arms manufactures sell their wares abroad to help finance purchases of technology. Avarice has replaced ideological principle in China's engagement with the world.

A Learning Curve

The nature of China's participation has also changed due to lessons learned. Foreigners have engaged in a huge educational effort to enhance China's understanding of and capacity in various international regimes. Chinese agencies and individuals have sought instruction, and the outside world has been glad to teach.[56] The messages that foreigners convey, however, are often discordant. International corporations and lawyers seek to convince the Chinese of the benefits of protecting intellectual property at the same time that Taiwanese, Korean, and Hong Kong businesspeople teach about the profits to be earned from IPR infringement. While the U.S. government lectures China on human rights, Lee Kwan Yew encourages China to ignore American advice. Norwegian, Indonesian, Kuwaiti, and American petroleum experts offered different advice on structuring joint venture agreements to explore and develop oil reserves.

Listening to this discordant advice, the Chinese have learned a great deal about international standards of conduct and how to evade them. In every realm, there are now policy communities in Beijing—though not in every provincial capital—that understand the international regimes China is joining. The intellectual gap between Beijing and the international community has narrowed, albeit more in some realms than others. The Chinese have learned how to extract the benefits that international regimes offer and minimize the costs they impose. Overall, then, China has become less distinctive. Its foreign policy calculus increasingly resembles that of other major powers.

A Changed International Environment

Since the late 1980s, a series of events has increased Beijing's sense of vulnerability: the tragedy of June 4, 1989, the Soviet Union's collapse, the Persian Gulf War, Taiwan's transition to democracy and the resulting enhanced international stature of the island, the growth of regional and multilateral forums in Asia, and the recent Japan-U.S. commitment to adjust their security alliance. China's leaders believe they have lost the diplomatic maneuverability and strategic value that the Cold War provided them. Asian regionalism deprives Beijing of opportunities to play one power against another. The collapse of Marxism-Leninism has increased China's susceptibility to potentially disruptive foreign ideas. Thus, despite the many gains China has secured in relations with the world and its greater involvement in international regimes, its leaders do not feel that their environment is clearly more hospitable and less threatening than in the mid-1980s.

At the same time, China's spectacular economic performance has generated confidence in the nation's long-term future. The economic factor helps explain their resistance on human rights abuses and their rejection of the notion of interdependence in the security realm. And it may contribute to increased Chinese caution and assertiveness as the leaders contemplate a larger role in world affairs. With such a record—especially in comparison to the abysmal record in the former Soviet Union—China's leaders naturally ask, "Why should we accept American advice on how to organize our country? The future may belong to us."

CONCLUSION: IMPLICATIONS AND RECOMMENDATIONS FOR AMERICAN CHINA POLICY

Secretary of State Madeleine Albright has stated that the United States has multifaceted interests with regard to China and that none of these prevails over all others. Our analysis lends weight to her observation. At the same time, U.S. policy must exhibit a sense of priorities.

The Objectives

The United States seeks a China that

- supports the peacekeeping functions of the United Nations;
- helps prevent the spread of weapons of mass destruction;
- contributes to the peace and stability of the Asia-Pacific region;
- promotes a liberal international trading system, manages its economy well so as to help sustain global growth, enters American markets in a nondisruptive fashion, and opens its markets to American products and services;
- allows the people of Hong Kong and Taiwan to enjoy peace, prosperity, and political freedom;
- participates in international efforts to protect the environment, combat terrorism, control narcotics trafficking, deter illegal population migration, and reduce the spread of communicable diseases;
- governs in an effective and humane fashion, cognizant of the people's needs and desires.

At this level of abstraction, the objectives largely coincide with those of the other industrial democracies and the countries of the Asia-Pacific region. As a result, since 1971 the United States and its partners in world affairs have pursued roughly similar China policies. The United States and its Asian and European partners have all recognized that while China's constructive involvement in world affairs does not guarantee success in the search for solutions to humanity's problems, its failure to participate would doom most efforts.

The Results

As our opening sections noted, while there have been serious setbacks and major impediments, great progress has been made. China is a more integral and constructive member of the world community today than it was 25, or 10, or 5 years ago. For the most part, it has not behaved in a disruptive fashion in the regimes it has joined. Unlike the Soviet Union, it has not formed a military bloc, organized a separate trading system with other nations, or sponsored an international revolutionary movement imbued with its ideology. Nor has it engaged in terrorist activities. To the contrary, our study pinpoints the many regimes in which China has become a valued member.

China's opening to the outside world and the outside world's welcome of it have proved largely beneficial to everyone concerned. Chinese development has narrowed the gap between the developed and the developing worlds, alleviating one of the greatest long-term sources of world tension. Americans have benefited from the new opportunities that its development offers. And despite China's continued and often harsh authoritarian rule, most Chinese people enjoy a higher standard of living and greater individual choice than at any point in modern history. The strategy begun 25 years ago is working.

The success of the strategy to involve China in the international system has intensified suspicion and opposition within China. Conservatives fear the hidden motive of the outside world is to subvert the Chinese political system through peaceful evolution, to hinder the country's economic growth, or to lock it into a subordinate position. They would like to thwart increased Chinese involvement in world affairs unless China unilaterally sets the terms. Other Chinese are less suspicious of the outside world's designs and even desire greater participation. But they believe that China is not yet sufficiently prepared and that deeper engagement will increase domestic tensions and threaten the country's fragile unity.

The strength of such thoughts among the top leaders and their advisers should not be underestimated. The history of modern China can be seen as oscillation between eras of eagerness to participate in the world and periods of resistance to the outside world. Some seek engagement, others fear it, and most wander ambivalently between the two camps. This helps explain China's hesitancy and prickliness in international negotiations. The Chinese interlocutors are either somewhat skeptical of the enterprise they are joining or have harsh critics peering over their shoulders. The outside world cannot take for granted positive Chinese responses to constructive Western overtures. The Chinese may have their own domestic reasons for rejecting them when they do so.

The Warning Signals

Our study offers ample warning signals that the situation could turn sour. Indeed, souring could already have begun to occur. Most recently, Beijing has bullied Hong Kong and Taiwan. It has increased its expenditures on modern weaponry and embarked on an ambitious program to purchase weapons and military technology from Russia. It has defended its territorial claims in the South China Sea through an enhanced military presence. It announced its adherence to the nuclear test ban agreement only after considerable external pressure. It has not meticulously and unambiguously fulfilled its nuclear nonproliferation pledges. China has frequently failed to meet commitments it has made in the commercial realm, such as controlling levels of exports and enforcing intellectual property rights. Its regulations governing foreign trade remain opaque despite repeated pledges to increase their transparency. China has intensified efforts to control communications across its borders (such as E-mail) and to prevent the telecommunications transformation from escaping government control (such as restricting use of satellite dishes). It has stepped up repression of political dissidents, nongovernmental trade union organizers, and religious people and their leaders worshipping and proselytizing without government license. And it has constrained foreign funding of purely scholarly research centers. This sobering list must be taken into account in formulating a realistic China policy.

American policy toward China must therefore go beyond the slogan of "constructive engagement" and recognition that American interests are multifaceted. Even though no single interest is overriding, American policy must display a sense of priorities and an understanding of the interrelationship among its many interests. A realistic China policy must provide satisfactory answers to three fundamental questions: What are the priorities? What strategies should be pursued to encourage China to participate constructively in world affairs? What precautionary measures should be taken in case that effort should fail? Our study provides several general and specific recommendations.

A Complex and Interrelated Agenda

Honest differences exist among Americans over the appropriate priorities in relations with China. Our Council study group contains adherents of all views.

Some argue that cooperation in the security and strategic realms realistically is a precondition for constructive participation in other areas. They note that only when China's leaders are convinced that their security interests are well served by an extensive involvement in world affairs will they permit cooperation in other areas to go forward. They argue that progress in securing China's cooperation was most rapid when the United States and China shared a strategic understanding about world affairs, and that partnership in various realms atrophied as this understanding eroded.

Adherents of this school also note that the fundamental issue is strategic: how to incorporate China's rising power into the established hierarchy of nations. Further, they observe that issues of war and peace take precedence in world affairs because only a stable world offers prospects for economic and political betterment. World order and human affairs are largely regulated through the strategic understandings and security arrangements reached among the major powers. No relationship will have greater impact for the United States in the decades ahead than that with China. The time to set relations on a firm path is now.

Others assign priority to economic development and hence the fostering of economic relations. They believe the quest for development prompts an emphasis on efficiency in the allocation of resources, which in turn requires a market economy. They argue that economic interdependence constrains aggressive external behavior. Economic development yields greater social diversity, produces an urban middle class that demands responsive governance, and brings about the liberating transportation and telecommunications transformations. Over the long run, therefore, the benefits of development are felt in the strategic and political domains.

Yet others stress primacy of the rule of law, human rights, or democratization. They argue that without these attributes, China will not be able to create a market economy and will not be a reliable partner in international security affairs. Leaders who deprive their own people of basic human and civil rights—rights guaranteed in the United Nations Universal Declaration of Human Rights—should not be allowed the benefits derived from participation in world affairs until they mend their ways. International recognition bestows legitimacy on such leaders at home and thereby perpetuates the dangers they pose to the world.

Finally, some would make cooperation on the problems of global interdependence—the so-called 21st-century issues of environment, health, migration, narcotics, and so on—the litmus test of China's credibility and reliability. These issues affect humanity's ability to survive on the planet, and therefore unmistakably affect China's own interests. They transcend national boundaries. If China is unwilling to assist in these spheres, the prospects of it cooperating in other areas are dim indeed.

All these views were eloquently expressed by various participants in our study. Each view, we find, has merit: security, trade, 21st-century issues, rule of law. While none should be neglected, no one area can claim enduring preeminence. Thus, we agree with Secretary of State Albright that progress in one area should not be hostage to progress in another. But the various areas are intertwined. Ultimately, failure to involve China in the regimes dealing with any of these areas will impede progress elsewhere. The implication is that the United States must seek a comprehensively constructive relationship with China. The agenda is a long and challenging one.

A Sense of Priorities

The United States seeks to influence a greater range of Chinese behavior than it has the capacity to affect. To aid the conduct of diplomacy and to provide the Chinese with sufficient guidance on the objectives of American policy, the United States must convey a sense of its priorities. They should be set early in the life of a new administration in Washington, and, barring major developments on the Chinese side, should be pursued at least for the lifespan of the administration. In the last few years, this has not been done.

American interests and Chinese behavior to date should help identify the priorities among American objectives. Our study suggests that for the foreseeable future, these are in the areas of security, economic relations, and encouragement of the rule of law.

In the security realm, China has yet to acknowledge the interdependent nature of security. Its leaders pursue Chinese security while engendering a sense of insecurity among potentially hostile neighbors. Eliciting Chinese cooperation to deter nuclear proliferation and an arms race in the Asian Pacific region clearly is a priority objective. In the economic domain, China resists some major domestic economic reforms, particularly of state-owned enterprises, that are vital to its continued progress in abiding by norms in trade and finance. It seeks unfettered access to American markets but remains protective of its own; it seems unconcerned about its growing trade surplus with the United States. Finally, Chinese officials claim to seek the rule of law while resisting establishment of the basic conditions for it. Without the rule of law, China's commerce will continue to rest on poorly regulated and insecure ground. Corruption will flourish. Moreover, unconstrained by law at home, rulers are more able to behave arbitrarily abroad. And the rule of law cannot be attained if Chinese citizens or foreigners remain vulnerable to opaque laws, arbitrary arrest, lengthy detention, lack of legal counsel, harsh imprisonment, and punishment by police answerable only to themselves or individual rulers.

These issues help identify the priority objectives for America's participation with China in international regimes: encouraging Chinese adherence to the International Atomic Energy Agency and the Missile Technology Control Regime standards in preventing the spread of nuclear technology, nuclear weapons, and advanced missiles and missile technology; eliciting its contribution, through multilateral and bilateral dialogue, to maintaining peace and stability in Korea, the East and South China Seas, the Taiwan Straits, and the Indochina peninsula; securing its membership in the WTO on terms that protect a liberal trading regime; and facilitating its development of the rule of law.

Multilateralism

The record demonstrates that American bilateral efforts are most effective when reinforced through multilateral efforts and supported by the bilateral efforts of others. The United States will not be successful if it unilaterally seeks to impose the conditions of China's involvement in world affairs. Integration proceeds best when there is an international consensus on the norms to which the outside world expects China to adhere. China's behavior in international financial markets, its eventual agreement to cease nuclear testing, the tempering of its assertiveness in the South China Sea, its assistance in bringing peace to Cambodia, and its endorsement of APEC goals to remove trade barriers are examples of the process at work.

Nevertheless, multilateralism cannot be a substitute for bilateral approaches. The institutions undergirding international regimes are frequently weak and unable to elicit compliance with their norms. In many regimes, there is no agreement on what norms should be respected. And American interests toward China do not entirely converge with those of its partners (see Appendix I).

The United States should consult widely with its Asian and European partners to secure as much support as possible for its priority objectives toward China. If the United States finds itself isolated on an issue, it should think twice about pressing the matter. The United States should also recognize that mutual adjustment is necessary to secure China's commitment. China should be able to help shape the rules that affect its interests.

Engaging in Strategic Dialogue

To repeat one of our most important findings: many top Chinese leaders reject the notion of interdependence and are relatively uninterested in fostering a shared perspective on world affairs. They see the world through very different eyes. But the record shows that when intensive, high-level, strategic dialogue with China's leaders was conducted in the 1970s and 1980s, progress was made in shaping Chinese thinking. Over time, Chinese perceptions can be influenced through dialogue, provided the Americans in their turn are willing to listen carefully to Chinese views. The dialogue cannot be a lecture.

After June 4, 1989, such consultations were drastically curtailed. That effort must be renewed. Specifically,

- At the highest levels, American efforts to adjust U.S. security treaties with Japan and South Korea in northeast Asia and to expand NATO eastward in Europe must be explained to China's leaders; the message should be that those changes are an important means of enhancing the stability of both regions by continuing to anchor Germany and Japan in an alliance system in Europe and Asia, respectively. Both efforts are intended to prevent the reappearance of age-old regional rivalries; neither is aimed against either Russia or China. Chinese leaders currently fear that the adjustments in the U.S.-Japan and U.S.-South Korea treaties are directed against them, as the Russians fear NATO expansion is directed against them. Unless these adjustments are well understood and accepted in Beijing and Moscow, their inadvertent result could be to provide a rationale for enhanced Russian-Chinese strategic cooperation.
- As to dialogue on strategic weapons, progress on START III would compel China (as well as Russia and the United States) to assess the role of nuclear weapons in the post-Cold War era. START III-level talks will almost certainly require the adoption of a minimum deterrence strategy by the United States, which would meet the conditions China has set for placing its nuclear forces on the negotiating table. At the same time, the United States should advance strategic nuclear arms talks among the Permanent Five to discourage China's nuclear force modernization.
- Military-to-military contact should be resumed and expanded to foster understanding and cooperation among air, naval, and ground forces. Technological exchanges should occur in areas such as mil-

itary medicine, surveillance of drug trafficking, disaster relief, conversion of military production to civilian uses, and force demobilization. Ship visits should occur regularly, including continuation of past patterns to Hong Kong. Discussions should be held on how to prevent accidental encounters in waters patrolled by both Chinese and American navies. Moreover, the United States should encourage Japanese self-defense forces and the South Korean military to engage in regular contact with the Chinese military. The objective is to help make China comfortable with the security environment that America's treaties with Japan and South Korea create.

- Dialogue is also required at the highest levels in the economic area. America's top economic officials should seek to elicit from their Chinese counterparts a better sense of their timetable for further economic reform. How do China's leaders foresee addressing their fundamental problems? And China's top economic officials deserve to hear American officials explain why China's early adherence to WTO standards would actually serve Chinese interests. As in the security realm, it is important for Chinese and American leaders, as well as leaders from industrial democracies other than America, to have a shared perspective concerning the trends in the world economy and how those trends can be shaped to serve the common interest. With this goal in mind, it seems appropriate to invite China to attend meetings of the Group of Seven.

- The U.S. government should continue a separate dialogue with China on human rights, one that is frank, vigorous, and rooted in mutual respect. The focus should not be on the release of specific dissidents, although those languishing in prison should not be forgotten; instead, the discussion should concentrate on how the two nations can cooperate such that each makes progress toward realizing the broad goals of the U.N. Declaration. The United States should encourage other industrial democracies to undertake their own, separate human rights discussions, recognizing that some of them, perhaps Canada, Australia, or Sweden, might elicit a more positive response.

Promoting Institutional Development

Institutional weakness impedes China's effective participation in many international regimes. The People's Republic lacks an adequate central revenue system, regular sources of local finance, a strong central banking system, a professional civil service, the effective rule of law, an independent judiciary, effective civilian control over the state, a robust system of representative assemblies, and a well-defined system of property rights.

Many Chinese officials desire to remedy these deficiencies, including encouragement of investigative journalism and formation of government-licensed nongovernmental organizations. International, regional, and national organizations, both governmental and nongovernmental, enjoy considerable opportunity to cooperate with China in all these realms. To cite some examples:

- The U.S. Arms Control and Disarmament Agency could be assigned an important role in arms control discussions. This would prompt the Chinese government to identify and strengthen its own agency. The Chinese have offered some arms control proposals. No harm would come from very tentatively exploring the details of their proposals.

- Cooperating with the State Science and Technology Commission Intellectual Property Rights Working Group would foster that agency's ability to enforce China's IPR regime.

- Chinese experts in the telecommunications and computer industries wish to learn about America's experience in restructuring its industries to benefit from the telecommunications revolution. Assistance in this realm would accelerate the dissemination of advanced communications technologies in China and the concomitant widening of access to information and to the outside world.

- The World Bank and the International Monetary Fund are providing advice on how to strengthen China's banking and revenue system. The U.N. Development Program is assisting the Chinese effort to create a national system of contested elections and secret balloting for the election of village leaders. Such efforts should be encouraged.

- Chinese officials have indicated their receptivity to dialogue on the fundamental issues of governance in the modern era: for example, the appropriate allocation of power between a central government and lower levels, the role of the state in the resolution of civilian disputes, the organization and role of representative assemblies, the provision of welfare for the unemployed and the elderly, and the regulation of property rights. Many Chinese recognize that their political system, like those of other countries, faces unprecedented challenges brought on by rapid technological change and economic growth. No country has a monopoly on wisdom concerning effective governance, and many Chinese officials are prepared to talk about their problems and their search for solutions.

The international community and the United States should seize upon these and many other similar opportunities. The quiet ferment in Chinese universities, research institutes, and at the intermediate and lower levels of the Chinese bureaucracy suggests China could be on the eve of considerable institutional change, and the United States could and should be part of that process to the extent opportunities arise for cooperation. Our study suggests that cooperation is strongest when the outside world reinforces and assists indigenously generated change.

Environment and Energy

The environmental and energy realms are so important that they deserve special mention. The United States must energetically assist international agencies such as the World Bank, the Asian Development Bank, and the U.N. Development Program in extending aid to China in these areas. The United States should lift its ban on U.S. assistance through the auspices of the U.S.-Asia Environment Partnership. This low-cost program could promote environmental protection in China and advance American business interests in selling environmental technologies.

Of primary concern to the United States and other countries, as well as to many Chinese, is China's rapidly increasing impact on global climate change. The United States should encourage China in the research and development of new energy efficiency and renewable energy technologies. It should smooth the transfer of such technologies, removing the constraints on government assistance to American vendors for trade development and private insurance in this realm. This is good for the global environment, good for business, and good for the health of the Chinese people.

In addition, training Chinese personnel in key bureaucracies such as the State Planning Commission and the National Environmental Protection Agency in areas like environmental economics is an inexpensive but highly effective means of assistance. Finally, as with trade issues, the United States should assist China's environmental system to become more transparent by aiding Chinese efforts to develop environmental databases and insisting on reporting requirements in global environmental accords.

Incentives, Sanctions, and Linkages

As with leaders anywhere, China's officials respond more favorably to incentives—payoffs and benefits—than to sanctions and the exacting of costs. Rewards can be distributed to build consensus; sanctions require allocating the costs internally, thereby creating disgruntled losers who become hostile to the outside world. It is better to concentrate on leading the Chinese to win-win situations while resisting their proclivity to insist on side payments for agreement to such solutions.

On the other hand, sanctions and linkages—when limited and credible—work. Chinese leaders engage in linkages and sanctions against other countries, and they respond to the threat or use of linkages and sanctions by others. The threat of a well-targeted and limited sanction, especially in the trade realm, is more effective, however, than efforts to link two broad and diverse areas of Chinese behavior (such as human rights performance and trade). Negotiation deadlines tied to the threat of sanctions are often the only way to force the Chinese coordinating agency to establish discipline among the several bureaucracies that make up a Chinese negotiating team. However, once an agreement has been reached and the sanctions averted, the recalcitrant bureaucracies may feel little obligation to adhere to the agreement unless they have received a payoff.

Establishing linkages between widely separated spheres of Chinese behavior is much more difficult, for example, by threatening withdrawal of China's most favored nation status because of its human rights record. Only officials at the highest levels in China have the authority to make the tradeoffs that such linkages require. Only they can issue binding and connected orders to such diverse bureaucratic domains as the public security apparatus and the manufacturing sector. And China's top leaders are unlikely to yield to such pressures frequently; their colleagues and subordinates would perceive them as weak. Moreover, by forcing such issues to the highest levels, the summit agenda becomes overloaded. Top leaders should not have to negotiate issues that are better handled quietly through bureaucratic channels. Their energies are best suited to the priority issues.

Behaving Credibly and Avoiding Hypocrisy

Our study stresses the essential rationality of China's leaders. Within the context of their domestic political situation and their perceptions of the international context, they seek to maximize their benefits and to minimize costs. The United States should therefore provide China's leaders with clear and consistent signals, indicating in credible fashion American objectives, capabilities, and strategies. Do not promise what cannot be delivered; do not issue empty threats; match words with deeds; and do not criticize China for behavior that the United States exhibits. The United States should not behave toward China in a hypocritical fashion, claiming its objective is to participate with China in international regimes on a mutually acceptable basis while acting unilaterally in global and regional affairs or not meeting its own international commitments. There are many examples of such discrepancies and none escapes Chinese attention. Specifically:

- The United States criticizes China's policy and behavior in the nuclear proliferation area but it has not acceded to the Chemical Weapons Convention, which China has joined.
- The United States decries Chinese violations of multilateral and bilateral sales agreements, but it has tested the limits of the arms sales agreement it reached with China in its sale of F-16s to Taiwan. The United States wants China to temper its weapons sales

and dual-use technology transfers in Asia—particularly in South Asia and the Middle East—lest the sales stimulate conflict, but it refuses to discuss how its own arms sales in Asia contribute to regional stability. The United States chastises Chinese arms salesmen for chasing profits, while its own sales have skyrocketed in recent years. The United States, let us remember, is the largest arms merchant in the world by far.

- The United States is handicapped in criticizing China's U.N. record when it is in arrears in meeting its own financial obligations to the United Nations.
- The United States' embrace of protectionist impulses encourages China to emulate it, while American support for a liberal trade regime, as with APEC and the WTO, places China under pressure to do the same.

In these instances, China's response to American inconsistencies is similar to that of most countries. It seizes upon them as justification for its own departure from norms. The United States places itself at a disadvantage in holding China's leaders accountable for their failure to adhere to their commitments and international norms. Greater consistency between rhetoric and action would enhance American credibility and effectiveness, not just with regard to China but elsewhere as well.

The Role of the Private Sector

The private sector greatly facilitates China's integration into the international system and its adherence to international norms. Universities, foundations, nongovernmental agencies, professional associations, and corporations are playing important roles in this area. Our study reveals, for instance, that the private sector has helped nurture the various policy communities in Beijing that now play pivotal roles in China's participation in each international regime: disarmament, environmental regulation, international banking, civil aviation, telecommunications, and even introduction of the rule of law.

Much more can be done. For example, business can play several vital roles in the environmental sphere:

- Most important, companies can lead by example by upholding high environmental standards. It is in their self-interest to do so, to avoid liability, for better public and investor relations, and because of competitive pressures. In addition, the International Standards Organization 14000 certification procedure will encourage Chinese businesses to become certified in order to qualify as vendors of goods and services to other companies. Foreign companies can share information on an informal basis and work with their Chinese counterparts through business associations to address common problems.
- With regard to human rights, the business community can employ quiet diplomacy, technical assistance, training, institution building, and grants to work with the Chinese government to improve the situation in areas of mutual interest including child labor, prison labor, women's rights, the independence of the judiciary, and the various elements of due process.

The Precautionary Measures

We have stressed that a forthcoming posture toward China cannot be guaranteed success. Serious warning signs indicate that it could fail. China could emerge as an assertive and disruptive force on the world scene. Or it could disintegrate, the chaos spilling over its borders and bringing turmoil to the region. The strategy outlined above is intended to minimize the chances of these outcomes. What precautionary measures are necessary? Our study prompts these recommendations:

- The strategies and tactics that China has used with such success in the early stages of its entry into international regimes, as well as its state-centric, zero-sum approach to many issues (especially in the security realm), dictate a hard-headed approach toward the country. Its leaders must be treated with dignity; to demean the leaders of such a great nation is inexcusable. But American negotiators must remain aware of Chinese tendencies to free-ride, to adopt an aggrieved posture to extract extra benefit, and to trade on unwarranted expectations of China's future strength. Such tactics should be vigorously resisted.

- This requires approaching China on the basis of American interests. All the policies recommended in our study flow from a sense of the American interest; they are intended to advance enlightened American purposes. Each American initiative must stand on its own merits. Generosity and well-intentioned offers of cooperation that only serve Chinese interests will be seized, but China will give little in return.
- The United States must retain a robust military presence in Asia, cultivate strong relations with Japan, South Korea, the ASEAN states, Australia, and New Zealand, and encourage the development of regional and sub-regional organizations. These measures are not aimed against China but rather at promoting regional stability. The web of regional, sub-regional, and bilateral ties exists to discourage disruptive behavior from any quarter.
- The United States must retain a full range of unofficial relations with Taiwan—political, economic, cultural, and military. While the United States has no obligation to support provocative Taiwan policies that predictably raise the mainland's ire, it has a moral and domestic legal obligation to ensure Taiwan has the capacity to sustain its self-defense. Shirking this responsibility would damage American credibility in Asia. The long-run American objective is clear: a peaceful reconciliation arranged by the two sides without duress.[57]
- China's entry into international regimes must occur on terms that protect the core purpose of the regime. This is particularly true for its negotiations to join the WTO.
- The United States must retain an independent capacity to understand Chinese domestic and foreign affairs. It must nurture a national capability to deal with China intelligently. This requires not allowing national analytical capabilities—especially in think tanks and universities—to become dependent on funding from China or Taiwan. The U.S. government must cultivate and reward expertise on China.

Rebutting the Skeptics

Many skeptics doubt that the course we recommend is workable.

They note the long-standing historical love-hate relationship between China and the United States: periods of mutual attraction, heightened expectations, and extensive cooperation followed by dashed hopes, mutual recriminations, and enmity. The skeptics assert that the two nations remain captive to the cycle.

Analysts differ over the explanations for the inability of the United States and China to sustain a constructive relationship. Some believe that the profound differences between the two civilizations preclude protracted cooperation: political and ideological differences intervene. As the two approach each other, their differences repel them.

Others claim that the differences in wealth, power, and global responsibilities inevitably engender divergent interests and perspectives. As a global power and a leader of the industrial democracies, the United States defends an international system it helped to create and that advances its interests, while China, as a rising power, seeks to change the established order. Tension and conflict are the predictable result.

Finally, some skeptics doubt the stability and the continuity of the Chinese system. They note that China is in a transition period whose outcome is uncertain. They urge the United States not to invest time, energy, and money in a Chinese elite and system that may not survive. They recommend cultivation of the next generation of leaders. But these skeptics overlook the fact that uncertainty about the leadership is a permanent feature of the Chinese political landscape, the successors cannot be identified, and the transition is likely to persist for several more decades.

All these cautionary notes have validity. They provide sober reminders of the enormous challenges ahead. They warn those dealing with China neither to harbor illusions nor to allow expectations to soar. But what is the appropriate response to these concerns? To look on China as a potential enemy and work to isolate, weaken, or divide it, thus helping to create what the United States should seek to avoid? Surely not. The United States and its partners traveled that road from 1949 to 1971, to no avail.

There is no real alternative to the course we recommend. As former Senator Sam Nunn declared in a recent speech, "Forewarned of the difficulties, the leaders of China and the United States must persist in forging cooperative bonds. . . . The future well-being of the American and Chinese people depends in large measure on the ability of the two nations to cooperate." The record suggests that enlightened self-interest on both sides will prevail, as has largely been the case since 1972, when China and the United States embarked on their epic journey to participate together in world affairs.

APPENDIX I: CONSULTING WITH AMERICA'S PARTNERS

The United States cannot successfully pursue a China policy that departs sharply from those of its partners in world affairs, especially the industrial democracies and the leading countries of Asia. Without their support, the United States would find itself isolated and the Chinese would slight American interests. Mobilization of partners' support requires constant consultation and policy coordination. This dimension of America's China policy has frequently been neglected.

For several reasons, however, the advice is easier to offer than to implement. America's European and Asian friends prefer to hide behind it. When consultations are carried out, Americans receive private assurances from foreign friends that they agree with American policy. Sometimes, the response is to be even more vigilant or resolute than Washington thinks wise. The Europeans and the Japanese, for example, privately encourage the U.S. government to pursue a firm line toward China on its entry into the WTO and on environmental issues. But after the United States has been encouraged to take the lead, its partners do not deliver an equally stern message to Beijing. They let Washington take the heat from the Chinese while they seek the commercial advantage that flows from a softer position.

China would also object to a concerted effort among the major powers to coordinate their policies toward it, as when the G-7 jointly decided on some sanctions after the tragedy of June 4, 1989. Beijing would perceive the effort as intended to isolate and contain China, and this perception would intensify its intransigence. Consultations must include China, and the American objective must be explained carefully to China's leaders.

Nor can the United States expect its partners readily to embrace its views on China's participation in world affairs. Frequently, Asian or European attitudes toward a particular regime differ from the American position. The United States has a more interventionist and activist view concerning human rights than most other countries. Its desire to place IPR and labor conditions on the WTO agenda is not matched by most others. It has taken the lead in trying to prevent nuclear proliferation. American foreign policy is simply more activist than that of the other industrial democracies. As a result, the United States will naturally seek to impose a higher standard for China's participation in an international regime than many allies in Europe or Asia will desire.

Further, America's interests in China frequently do not coincide with those of its global partners. The countries of Western Europe lack the regional security interests that the United States possesses, and they do not share America's historical and moral obligations toward Taiwan. Nor do the Western Europeans have the intense missionary impulse toward China that is deeply rooted in the American approach. The United States has sought to make China Christian, liberal, or democratic for nearly 150 years. While Europeans have occasionally exhibited the same tendencies, they have been more likely to view China with greater detachment and less ideological zeal. Their interest is primarily economic.

As an immediate and huge neighbor, China is more central to Japan's interests than it is to those of the United States. For most of American history, China has been a peripheral or secondary concern, but it has always been central to Japan. Its cultural and political influence on Japan has been enormous.

Today Japanese tend to harbor deeply ambivalent sentiments toward China.[58] They consider it an important market and source of raw materials, but are frustrated by the difficulties of doing business there. They feel remorse for Japan's brutal aggression and occupation of Manchuria and much of China from 1931 to 1945, but resent China's continued bitterness and refusal to forgive. They acknowledge the richness and antiquity of Chinese civilization from which Japan has borrowed so heavily, but are smug in the knowledge that their technology and economy are now far superior. They welcome the prosperity and stability that China's rapid economic growth has contributed to the region, but fear the possible harmful military and environmental consequences for Japan. They are disturbed by China's human rights abuses, but are even more concerned that social instability in China could spill across its borders and bring turmoil to the entire region.

Japan wishes neither to antagonize its huge neighbor nor become its captive in a tight embrace. All these considerations prompt a cautious, deliberate, and quiet posture toward China. Japan's interests with regard to China are so great that Tokyo is no longer willing to surrender control over its China policy to the United States, as it quite literally did in the 1950s and 1960s. But it is also unwilling to depart sharply from American policy. Its preference is for a division of labor in which the United States bears the primary burden of dealing with China on the contentious issues, such as Taiwan, nuclear proliferation, and the removal of trade barriers, while Japan financially assists China in solving its environmental problems and alleviating its economic bottlenecks. Japan, of course, would benefit economically from this division of labor.

There is a strong desire throughout East Asia for the United States to provide a balance to China's military power, but the desire is not clearly voiced because of concern that the United States will not sustain the role. Few wish to be identified in the Chinese mind as an American lackey, especially if the United States is eventually going to withdraw its military from the region and China emerges as the dominant power.

In short, the United States must consult with its partners and ensure that its China policy on the whole converges with the policies of its allies. But it must do so in ways that do not arouse Chinese fears of encirclement. To elicit cooperation from America's Asian partners requires quelling Asian concerns about U.S. constancy and credibility. And because the United States' interests and responsibilities sometimes diverge from the views of those in Europe and East Asia, America's China policy must occasionally be a singular effort.

APPENDIX II: HONG KONG

China's international reputation and domestic evolution depend heavily on the fate of Hong Kong. In the 1984 Sino-British Declaration on the future of Hong Kong, China pledged that Hong Kong would retain its own economic, political, and social system after it returned to Chinese rule on July 1, 1997. The Chinese slogan of "one country, two systems" formulated by Deng Xiaoping indicated how the central government in Beijing would rule Hong Kong.

If China adheres to its commitment, it will have taken a giant step in its integration into the international economic and political system. It will have demonstrated that it can rule one of the world's great cities effectively. And its own internal development will be greatly accelerated because of the increased confidence of the outside world in China's credibility.

Background

The transfer of Hong Kong from British to Chinese sovereignty is a genuinely historic event. Combined with the return of Macau to Chinese rule in 1999, Hong Kong's transfer terminates China's colonial experience. Indeed, with the lowering of the Union Jack in Hong Kong and the Portuguese flag in Macau, for the first time in 400 years, no foreign colony will exist in East, Southeast, or South Asia. Asia's encounter with Western imperialism has ended.

The British obtained the island of Hong Kong in 1842 to facilitate commerce with China, including the sale of opium. The British secured adjacent territory on two additional occasions, the last in 1898 through a 99-year lease.

Throughout 157 years of rule, the British governed Hong Kong as a colony. The governor was appointed in London without extensive consultation with the populace of Hong Kong. Until recently the top civil servants were British. The major companies in the colony—Jardines, Butterfield and Swire, the Hong Kong and

Shanghai Bank, and so on—were in British hands. The British preserved Hong Kong's tranquillity by preventing China's warring factions from extending their turmoil and strife into the colony. Neither the communists nor the nationalists operated openly, and British intelligence monitored and disrupted their covert activities. The British maintained a delicate balance between individual liberty and social order. Only in the last five years of their rule, after agreeing to its return to China, did they aspire to turn Hong Kong into a genuine democracy.

Hong Kong's transfer to Chinese sovereignty is an unusual ending to a colonial experience. Most former colonies around the world emerged as independent countries when the imperial power withdrew. Moreover, Hong Kong is being handed over to China without the opinion of its inhabitants being elicited. Britain had little choice in the matter; China would have objected had Britain sought to give Hong Kong residents the right to self-determination. As a result, the destiny of a people who enjoy considerable liberty is being placed in the hands of China's authoritarian rulers.

Conflicting Perspectives

To many in the West, the transfer of a free people to communist jurisdiction without consultation betrays the principle of self-determination. The transfer seems to go against recent global trends away from communist dictatorships and toward democracy. Many observers in the United States and Western Europe, therefore, view the transfer with a tinge of regret and apprehension. Yet Britain had no realistic alternative, since its 99-year lease on the vast portion of the territory expired in 1997. China had the legal right to reclaim the territory, and its rulers were intent on exercising that right.

In the minds of most mainland Chinese, Hong Kong's sordid origins and the enlargement of the British territory during China's military weakness in the 19th century were a source of humiliation. The return to Chinese rule is an occasion for national celebration. To most Asians, and especially to most Chinese, the event is congruent with global trends: the erosion of Western influence, the end of imperialism, and the rise of Asia and China in world affairs. And most Hong Kong dwellers view the transfer with mixed emotions.

The Challenge

The 1984 Joint Declaration and the subsequent Basic Law on the governance of Hong Kong passed by the National People's Congress in 1990 contain many ambiguous phrases that have yet to be clarified. But the underlying spirit of the two documents is clear. Hong Kong will be a Special Administrative Region within the People's Republic of China. Hong Kong will be ruled by people from Hong Kong. It should enjoy a high degree of autonomy under nominal Beijing rule. It will, for example, retain its own legal system, have its own legislature, issue its own currency, control the flow of people across its borders, maintain its own civil service, and enter into its own international commercial agreements.

Considerable doubt exists, however, as to whether Hong Kong will in fact enjoy the autonomy that the "one country, two systems" formula implies. The formula suggests that Beijing will be willing to tolerate activities in Hong Kong that it would not permit in the rest of the PRC. During the 48 years of Communist Party rule, after all, Beijing's instinctive reaction to developments it does not like usually has been to assert its authority and bring matters under control.

Hong Kong's future has been complicated by the rancorous relationship that developed between the government of Hong Kong and the authorities in Beijing following the arrival of Governor Christopher Patten in 1992. Patten immediately and openly sought to accelerate the pace of democratization in Hong Kong and to extend the civil liberties the populace enjoyed. His initiatives were supported by a substantial portion of the Hong Kong population, even though many objected to the brash manner in which he pursued his objectives. He almost courted Chinese animosity.

Indeed, Beijing soon complained that Patten had ignored British commitments and private understandings that the Chinese government had reached with the British Foreign Ministry. The charge has considerable merit, as does Patten's claim that the Chinese refused to conduct serious negotiations with him after his public pronouncements.

The result of the Patten-Beijing rift was that Patten pushed ahead with changes in the Hong Kong political system between 1992 and 1997, such as the introduction of a democratically elected Legislative Council and a revised Civil Liberties Ordinance. And China's leaders made clear that they did not accept these changes and would abolish them after July 1, 1997.

This history has rendered judgments about Beijing's credibility difficult. By what standards is one to judge Beijing's adherence to its international commitments—by the claims of the outgoing British colonial administrators or by how the Chinese interpret their international agreements? And is the Hong Kong system to be preserved that of 1990 or 1997?

Preserving Hong Kong's Autonomy

But the big issues concern not so much the end game between the British and the Chinese as the construction of Hong Kong's new government under its first chief executive, C. H. Tung. Selected in December 1996, Tung emerged as Hong Kong's leader through a competitive and consultative but not democratic process; the process, orchestrated by Beijing, included broad sectors of Hong Kong society but pointedly excluded political activists who vociferously endorsed Patten's reforms.

Tung now bears the burden of molding a system that will protect Hong Kong's autonomy. Among his major political and economic challenges are these:

- To ensure his political preeminence in the Hong Kong political landscape, and to secure deference from the many mainland political figures who will be based in Hong Kong: the head of the newly established Ministry of Foreign Affairs office, the head of the New China News Agency, the first secretary of the Hong Kong branch of the Chinese Communist Party (whether it continues underground or surfaces), and the commander of the People's Liberation Army forces based in Hong Kong;
- To enjoy immediate and unfettered access to the highest rulers in Beijing without passing through intermediate bureaucrats, to have a status higher than that of ministers and provincial chief-

tains, to identify a sympathetic Politburo member who will manage the Hong Kong portfolio within the central government, and to be able to participate in meetings in Beijing in which the highest leaders consider issues affecting Hong Kong's fate;

- To maintain the autonomy, neutrality, and professionalism of Hong Kong's civil service, and to ensure that recruitment and promotions are based on merit and not political considerations;
- To maintain the rule of law and an independent judiciary and to ensure that the roles of the police and military forces in Hong Kong are decided by the Hong Kong government;
- To protect the freedom of access to and dissemination of information, essential to Hong Kong's prosperity and market economy;
- To sustain the international nature of Hong Kong's cultural and social life by preserving the international quality of the universities, the integrity of the press, and the people's religious freedom;
- To protect the value of the Hong Kong dollar, to defend the integrity of the banking system, and to retain control over the foreign currency reserves that provide Hong Kong's credibility as a storehouse of value;
- To sustain the fragile arrangements that enable the market economy to flourish.

If China permits Tung to achieve all the above objectives, the special administrative region will prosper. If China interferes and deprives the new government of sufficient authority to maintain Hong Kong's confidence in its future well-being, deep troubles will arise.

The transition will not be easy or entirely smooth. Not everyone wants "one country, two systems" to work. For instance, some elements in Taiwan may fear that a very successful transition will place Taiwan under additional pressure to reach an accommodation with the mainland, while a disastrous takeover could increase the world's support for the emergence of an independent Taiwan. Or some Hong Kong residents may seek a greater degree of democracy than the new government is prepared to grant, at least initially, out of concern that the freedom will be used to subvert the mainland government. As with any new administration, moments of uncertainty and difficulty are bound to arise, as Hong Kong's new leaders feel their way forward.

Chinese patience and forbearance will be tested at such moments. If China's leaders rise to the occasion, they will provide a resounding answer to the underlying question posed in this study. The recovery of Hong Kong offers them the opportunity to demonstrate that they adhere to their commitments and that they can act responsibly in regional and international affairs. A successful transition will greatly accelerate China's entry into the international economic and political system and encourage the outside world's participation in China's development. A failed transition would be a major setback to China's constructive involvement in world affairs and to Sino-American relations.

U.S. Policy

Responsibility for a successful transition rests primarily with the new government of Hong Kong special administrative region, the outgoing colonial government, Beijing, and the British. But the United States and the entire region have a major interest in Hong Kong's continued prosperity. It would not be easy to replace Hong Kong in its valuable role as a crossroads between China and the rest of the world. Hong Kong facilitates China's economic and political development. For all these reasons, the United States government, acting in concert with its friends and allies, should stress:

- To the democratic forces in Hong Kong, their participation in the new special administrative region will enhance its prospects for democratic rule and continuation of civil liberties;
- To China, the American welcome of the end of China's colonial era, the importance that the United States attaches to China's adherence to agreements on Hong Kong, and the damage that would occur to Sino-American relations if China transgresses those agreements;
- To Taiwan, the benefits it would derive from Hong Kong's suc-

cessful transition and the importance of its refraining from activities that would destabilize the transition;

- To the new leaders of Hong Kong, the desire and intent of the United States that their government retain the qualities that have contributed to Hong Kong's remarkable tranquillity, prosperity, and liberty;
- To the outgoing government of Hong Kong and Great Britain, American admiration for the economic and political legacy they leave. Future historians will note that, at the end, they sought to create a democracy. They should extend a helping hand to their successors, and after July 1, vigilantly monitor China's adherence to its 1984 agreement.

NOTES

1. These statistics are based on the official exchange rate, which Nicholas Lardy argues yields too high an overall assessment of Chinese trade as a percentage of GNP. Notes on file with authors.
2. This picture may be somewhat exaggerated, since much trade and investment with Hong Kong and many pledged joint ventures never materialize. Moreover, over 50 percent of China's foreign direct investment is in Hong Kong.
3. Michael D. Swaine, "China and Arms Control," in Michel Oksenberg and Elizabeth Economy, eds, *Participating with China in World Affairs* (New York: Council on Foreign Relations Press, forthcoming), pp. 29–35.
4. Margaret M. Pearson, *Joint Ventures in the People's Republic of China: The Control of Foreign and Direct Investment under Socialism* (Princeton: Princeton University Press, 1991); Susan Shirk, *How China Opened Its Door: The Political Success of the PRC's Foreign Trade and Investment Reforms* (Washington: Brookings Institution, 1994); Nicholas Lardy, "China and the International Financial System," in Oksenberg and Economy; and Michael J. Moser and Jesse T. H. Chang, *Foreign Trade, Investment, and the Law in the People's Republic of China* (London: Oxford University Press, 1987).
5. Lardy in Oksenberg and Economy, *Participating with China*, p. 12.
6. Ibid., p. 19.
7. Nina Halpern, "Information Flows and Policy Coordination in the Chinese Bureaucracy," in Kenneth Lieberthal and Michael Lampton, eds., *Bureaucracy, Politics and Decision-Making in Post-Mao China (Berkeley: University of California Press, 1992)*, pp. 125–148; Carol Lee Hamrin, "The Party Leadership System," in Lieberthal and Lampton, pp. 95–124; and Joseph Fewsmith, *Dilemmas of Reform in China: Political Conflict and Economic Debate* (Armonk: M.E. Sharpe, 1994).
8. Michel Oksenberg, Pitman Potter, and William B. Abnett, *China and the IPR Issue: Analysis and Policy Recommendations* (Prepared for the National Bureau of Asian Research, 1996).
9. Alexander H. Platt, "China's Progress toward Integration into the International Civil Aviation Regime," in Oksenberg and Economy, *Participating with China*, pp. 6–7.
10. Samuel Kim, "China and the United Nations," in Oksenberg and Economy, *Participating with China*, pp. 31–32; and Michel Oksenberg and Elizabeth Economy, "China: Implementation under Economic Growth and Market Reform," in Edith Brown Weiss and Harold Jacobson, eds., *Engaging Countries:*

Strengthening Compliance with International Environmental Accords (Cambridge: Massachusetts Institute of Technology Press, forthcoming).
11. Kim in Oksenberg and Economy, *Participating with China*, quoting Hao Yufan, *Environmental Protection and Chinese Foreign Policy* (Washington, D.C.: American Enterprise Institute, 1992), p. 166.
12. Andrew J. Nathan, "China and the International Human Rights Regime," in Oksenberg and Economy, pp. 8–9.
13. Li Wei, *The Security Service for Chinese Central Leaders* (Unpublished manuscript, 1994). See also Kenneth Lieberthal, *Governing China: From Revolution through Reform* (New York: W.W. Norton, 1995).
14. Richard Baum, "Modernization and Legal Reform in Post-Mao China: The Rebirth of Socialist Legality," in *Studies in Comparative Communism*, 19, no. 2 (Summer 1986).
15. Ko-Yung Tung, "Law and Legal Regime in China" in Oksenberg and Economy.
16. Stanley Lubman, "The Future of Chinese Law," in *The China Quarterly*, no. 141 (March 1995).
17. Hamrin in Lieberthal and Lampton, pp. 94–124; A. Doak Barnett, *The Making of Foreign Policy in China: Structure and Process* (Boulder: Westview Press, 1985); David Shambaugh, "China's National Security Research Bureaucracy," in *The China Quarterly*, 110 (June 1987), pp. 276–304; and Carol Lee Hamrin, "Elite Politics and the Development of China's Foreign Policy," in Thomas Robinson and David Shambaugh, eds., *Chinese Foreign Policy and Practice* (London: Oxford University Press, 1994).
18. Kim, in Oksenberg and Economy, p. 32; and Alastair Iain Johnston, "Learning versus Adaptation: Explaining Change in Chinese Arms Control Policy in the 1980s and 1990s," *The China Journal*, no. 35 (January 1996), pp. 36–43.
19. Frederick S. Tipson, "China and Telecommunications," in Oksenberg and Economy, p. 2.
20. Nathan, in Oksenberg and Economy, pp. 10–14.
21. Ibid., p. 3.
22. Ibid., p. 12.
23. Tipson, in Oksenberg and Economy, p. 27.
24. Ibid., p. 32.
25. Michael D. Swaine, "China and Arms Control," in Oksenberg and Economy, p. 3.
26. Ibid.
27. Ibid., p. 30, quoting Alastair Iain Johnston, "Learning versus Adaptation."
28. Harold K. Jacobson and Michel Oksenberg, *China and the Keystone International Economic Organizations* (Ann Arbor: Institute for Social Research, 1987).
29. Swaine, in Oksenberg and Economy, p. 3.
30. Ibid., pp. 3–4.

31. Ibid., pp. 16–17.
32. Ibid., p. 14.
33. Nathan in Oksenberg and Economy, pp. 22–23.
34. Ibid., p. 25.
35. Ibid., 32.
36. Shirk, *How China Opened Its Door.*
37. Pearson, in Oksenberg and Economy, p. 11.
38. Nicholas Lardy, "The Role of Foreign Trade and Investment in China's Economic Transformation," *China Quarterly* (December 1995), p. 1,074.
39. Oksenberg, Potter, and Abnett, *China and the IPR Issue.*
40. Lardy in Oksenberg and Economy, pp. 31–33.
41. Ibid., p. 20.
42. Ibid., pp. 7, 22.
43. Ibid., p. 13.
44. Ibid., p. 18.
45. Ibid., p. 13.
46. Oksenberg, Potter, and Abnett, pp. 12–24. For more information, see Tipson in Oksenberg and Economy.
47. Todd M. Johnson, "Foreign Involvement in China's Energy Sector," in Oksenberg and Economy, pp. 14–15.
48. Ibid., p. 18.
49. Ibid.; Abigail Jahiel, *Policy Implementation under Socialist Reform: The Case of Water Pollution Management in the People's Republic of China* (Ann Arbor: University of Michigan Press, 1994); Kenneth G. Lieberthal and David M. Lampton, *Bureaucracy, Politics, and Decision Making in Post-Mao China*; and Oksenberg and Economy in Weiss and Jacobson, *Engaging Countries.*
50. Kim, in Oksenberg and Economy, p. 39.
51. Ibid., p. 25.
52. Ibid., p. 16.
53. For more extensive analysis, see especially Robinson and Shambaugh, *Chinese Foreign Policy and Practice*; Samuel Kim, *China and the World* (Boulder: Westview, 1989).
54. Michael Swaine, *China: Domestic Change and Foreign Policy* (Santa Monica: RAND Press, 1995).
55. Lucian W. Pye, *Chinese Negotiating Style: Communist Approaches and Cultural Principles* (New York: Quorum Books, 1992); Richard H. Solomon, *Chinese Political Negotiating Behavior: A Briefing Analysis* (Santa Monica: RAND Press, 1985); and Alfred D. Wilhelm, *The Chinese at the Negotiating Table: Style and Characteristics* (Washington, DC: National Defense University Press, 1994).
56. David Zweig and Chen Changgui, *China's Brain Drain to the United States: Views of Overseas Chinese Students and Scholars in the 1990s* (Berkeley: Regents of the University of California, 1995); and David M. Lampton, *A Relation-*

ship Restored: Trends in U.S.-China Educational Exchanges, 1978–1984 (Washington, D.C.: National Academy Press, 1986).

57. See also Michel Oksenberg, "Taiwan, Tibet, and Hong Kong in Sino-American Relations," in Ezra Vogel, ed. *China-U.S. Relations in the Twenty-First Century: Fostering Cooperation, Preventing Conflict* (New York, W.W. Norton, 1997).
58. Allen S. Whiting, *China Eyes Japan* (Berkeley: University of California Press, 1989); Gerald Segal, "The Coming Confrontation Between China and Japan," *World Policy Journal*, vol. 10, no. 2 (Summer 1993); and Zakaria Haji Ahmad, "Japan and China in Pacific Asia's Evolving Security Environment," *Global Affairs*, vol. 8, no. 1 (Winter 1993).

MEMBERS OF THE STUDY GROUP

Shaping U.S.-China Relations does not necessarily reflect the opinions of any study group participant or sponsor.

CHARLES N. ANDREAE is President, Andreae, Vick and Associates, LLC

LISA B. BARRY is Director, International Trade Policy, The Boeing Company

ROBERT L. BERNSTEIN is Chairman, Human Rights Watch

JAN BERRIS is Vice President, National Committee on U.S.-China Relations

DAVID J. BIGGS is Associate Political Affairs Officer, Department of Political Affairs, United Nations

CARROLL BOGERT is International Correspondent, *Newsweek*

MARY BROWN BULLOCK is President, Agnes Scott College

RICHARD BUSH is National Intelligence Officer for East Asia, National Intelligence Council

LAURA B. CAMPBELL is Director, Environmental Law International

ELIZABETH ECONOMY is Fellow for China, Council on Foreign Relations

*Individual wrote a paper for the Study Group.

KARL W. EIKENBERRY is Senior Country Director for China and Mongolia, Office of the Secretary of Defense

HART FESSENDEN is Adjunct Professor, Stern School of Business, New York University

WENDY FRIEMAN is Director, Asia Technology Program, SAIC

HARRY HARDING is Dean, Elliott School of International Affairs, George Washington University

ROBERT M. HATHAWAY is International Relations Committee, U.S. House of Representatives

*MIKKAL E. HERBERG is Director, Emerging Markets, ARCO

RICHARD HEROLD is Director, International Government Relations, Amoco Corporation

MERIT E. JANOW is Professor in the Practice of International Trade, School of International and Public Affairs, Columbia University

*TODD M. JOHNSON is Environmental Economist, The World Bank

*ALASTAIR IAIN JOHNSTON is John L. Loeb Associate Professor of the Social Sciences, Harvard University

ROBERT A. KAPP is President, United States-China Business Council

ANDREW BYONGSOO KIM, CFA, is President, Sit/Kim International Investors Associates, Inc.

*SAMUEL S. KIM is Adjunct Professor of Political Science and Senior Research Scholar, East Asian Institute, Columbia University

JAMES KLURFELD is Editorial Page Editor, *Newsday*

DINAH LEE KÜNG is Co-Chair, Press Freedom Committee, Overseas Press Club

DAVID M. LAMPTON is President, National Committee on U.S.-China Relations

JOHN D. LANGLOIS is Managing Director, J.P. Morgan & Co., Incorporated

*NICHOLAS R. LARDY is Senior Fellow, The Brookings Institution

TERRILL E. LAUTZ is Vice President, Henry Luce Foundation

KENNETH LIEBERTHAL is Arthur Thurnau Professor of Political Science, William Davidson Professor of International Business, University of Michigan

ERIC P. LIU is Commentator, MSNBC

DANIEL C. LYNCH is Visiting Fellow, Pacific Council on International Policy

DOUGLAS P. MURRAY is President, Lingnan Foundation

*ANDREW J. NATHAN is Professor of Political Science, Columbia University

MICHEL OKSENBERG is Senior Fellow, Asia Pacific Research Center, Stanford University

STEPHEN ORLINS is Senior Advisor, AEA Investors, Inc.

SUSAN WILLIAMS O'SULLIVAN is Senior Regional Affairs Officer/China, Bureau of Democracy, Human Rights and Labor, U.S. Department of State

MAYNARD PARKER is Editor, *Newsweek*

*MARGARET M. PEARSON is Associate Professor, Department of Government and Politics, University of Maryland

LINDA J. PERKIN is Deputy Director, Department of Political Affairs, West Asia Division, United Nations

*ALEXANDER PLATT is Executive Vice President, Projects International, Inc.

ROBERT S. PRICE, JR. is Director, International Relations, U.S. Department of Energy

ARTHUR H. ROSEN is President Emeritus, National Committee on U.S.-China Relations

*LESTER ROSS is Attorney, Paul, Weiss, Rifkind, Wharton & Garrison

ENID C.B. SCHOETTLE is Consultant, Department of Humanitarian Affairs, United Nations

DANIEL A. SHARP is President, The American Assembly

ANN B. SLOANE is Principal, Sloane & Hinshaw, Inc.

RICHARD J. SMITH is Deputy National Intelligence Officer for Global and Multilateral Issues, National Intelligence Council

ALLAN Y. SONG is Director of Asia Programs, United Nations Association-U.S.A.

*MICHAEL D. SWAINE is Senior Researcher, RAND

*FREDERICK S. TIPSON is International Public Affairs Vice President, AT&T

MAYNARD TOLL is Chairman, Edmund S. Muskie Foundation

JAMES T.B. TRIPP is General Counsel, Environmental Defense Fund

*KO-YUNG TUNG is Senior Partner, O'Melveny & Myers

CASIMIR A. YOST is Director, Institute for the Study of Diplomacy, Georgetown University

ALICE YOUNG is Partner and Chair, Asia Pacific Practice, Kaye, Scholer, Fierman, Hays & Handler

DAVID ZWEIG is Associate Professor, Hong Kong University of Science and Technology